Hastenbeck 1757

The French Army and the Opening Campaign of the Seven Years War

Olivier Lapray

Translated by William Raffle

Helion & Company

Helion & Company Limited
Unit 8 Amherst Business Centre
Budbrooke Road
Warwick
CV34 5WE
England
Tel. 01926 499619
Email: info@helion.co.uk
Website: www.helion.co.uk
Twitter: @helionbooks
Visit our blog at http://blog.helion.co.uk/

Published by Helion & Company 2021
Designed and typeset by Mach 3 Solutions Ltd (www.mach3solutions.co.uk)
Cover designed by Paul Hewitt, Battlefield Design (www.battlefield-design.co.uk)

Original text © Olivier Lapray and first published in French as *Campagne de 1757 en Westphalie*; translation by William Raffle © Helion and Company 2021
Illustrations © as individually credited
Colour uniform plates by Patrice Courcelle, © Helion and Company 2021
Maps by George Anderson © Helion and Company 2021

Cover: Figure: Fusilier, Régiment de Picardie (artwork by Patrice Courcelle, © Helion and Company 2021); background: 'Camp de Frinquen', copper engraving by Jacob van der Schley (Public Domain)

Every reasonable effort has been made to trace copyright holders and to obtain their permission for the use of copyright material. The author and publisher apologise for any errors or omissions in this work, and would be grateful if notified of any corrections that should be incorporated in future reprints or editions of this book.

ISBN 978-1-914059-80-3

British Library Cataloguing-in-Publication Data.
A catalogue record for this book is available from the British Library.

All rights reserved. No part of this publication may be reproduced, stored in a retrieval system, or transmitted, in any form, or by any means, electronic, mechanical, photocopying, recording or otherwise, without the express written consent of Helion & Company Limited.

For details of other military history titles published by Helion & Company Limited, contact the above address, or visit our website: http://www.helion.co.uk

We always welcome receiving book proposals from prospective authors.

Contents

Introduction ... iv

1 The French Army in 1757 ... 7
2 The Beginning of the Seven Years War ... 14
3 Assembly on the Rhine ... 18
4 Between the Rhine and the Lippe ... 28
5 The Main Operation ... 42
6 On the Other Side of the Weser ... 57
7 Entry Into Saxony ... 65
8 Plan of Attack – 26 July ... 82
9 The Battle of Hastenbeck ... 91
Epilogue ... 114

Appendices
I   Order of Battle of the Armée du Bas Rhin ... 120
II   State of the Armée du Bas Rhin, 1 July 1757 ... 126
III   Maréchal d'Estrées' Camp at Frenke on 24 & 25 July 1757 ... 129
IV   Battle of Hastenbeck 26 July 1757: Order of Battle of the Infantry of *Maréchal* d'Estrées' Armée du Bas Rhin ... 130
V   Battle of Hastenbeck 26 July 1757: Order of Battle of the Duke of Cumberland's Left Wing of the Army of Observation ... 132
VI   Formation of the Head of the Column which Attacked the Hastenbeck Woods ... 134
VII   French Losses from the Battle of Hastenbeck ... 136
VIII Memoir of the Comte de Maillebois and Clarifications Presented to the King by *Maréchal* d'Estrées ... 141

Select Bibliography ... 143

Introduction

If war 'is the premeditated and methodical struggle of two parties which, with the help of their armed forces, strive to achieve a political goal,' then as Clausewitz wrote, war is simply 'the continuation of policy by other means'.[1]

In war, victory is gained when an adversary is defeated. One side is defeated when they cannot react to their adversary, for example if they cannot oppose a manoeuvre. Causes of this can be lack of space, lack of resources, or lack of command. On a tactical level, if a force must abandon a position, has no more ammunition, has suffered excessive losses, or is no longer able to face combat from the poor morale of troops or their leaders, these are also major causes of defeat.

From the eighteenth century, writers and strategists sought to identify unchanging principles through historical study which would achieve victory on the battlefield and so benefit the campaign as a whole. These immutable principles would guide the preceding decision and generate the manoeuvre, an action planned in time and space, in order to achieve the objective. Whether these unchanging principles exist or not, one quickly understands that the central element of all the combinations is the military leader who is the origin of the decisions made.

'A man of war must have as much character as wit' wrote Napoleon in his observations on the campaign of 1799. He explained that the French commander in question 'lacked neither wit nor courage, he lacked character; he spoke of the war boldly but vaguely; he was not fit to lead'.[2]

Antoine de Jomini specified the two great qualities expected of the military leader as 'great character, or moral courage, which leads to great resolutions, then the coolness or physical courage which overcomes dangers'.[3] The general's ability and force of will become manifest in their manoeuvres and ultimately lead to victory or defeat in the battle or campaign.

---

1 Wilhelm Rustöw, in Captain Ernest Raymond Henry, *Essai d'un abrégé de philosophie de la guerre* (Paris: Dumaine, 1879), p.15. Carl von Clausewitz, *De la guerre* (Perrin: Librairie académique, 1999), p.32.
2 Henri Gatien Bertrand, *Guerre d'Orient. Campagnes d'Égypte et de Syrie, 1798-1799: mémoires pour servir à l'histoire de Napoléon* (Paris: Comptoir des Imprimeurs-Unis, 1847), Vol.II, p.230
3 Antoine-Henri Jomini, *Précis de l'art de la guerre* (Brussels: Librraie Militaire de J-B Petit, 1841), Vol.II, p.44.

Military history is therefore primarily the history of military leaders and, more generally, of command. Count Turpin de Crissé reported that *Maréchal* de Saxe 'meeting a grenadier who was a very handsome soldier, told him it would be desirable that the King had a hundred thousand men like him. The grenadier answered him – it would be much better if he had two like you'.[4]

Under Louis XIV, 'the frequent presence of the King in the armies excited the loyalty of the marshals and helped to resolve thorny questions of hierarchy and the organization of command'.[5] Under the reign of Louis XV, the exercise of command became more complex. War, freed from problems of territorial possession, was motivated by objectives beyond military affairs. Its actions had political origins, extensions and, in the absence of the King from the army, the appointment of the *général-en-chef* was also a matter of domestic policy.

The Seven Years War saw new alliances and the simultaneous conduct of military operations in several theatres. This time saw the beginnings of military strategy and tactics. The campaign of 1757 involved an army of 100,000 men, witnessed large-scale manoeuvres and with it the necessary operational corollaries of supply and resupply. The campaign also testified to the difficulty of exercising command in the face of a court and a government for which short-term results took precedence over long-term considerations.

The campaign of the French armies in Westphalia saw its outcome play out around the village of Hastenbeck, on 26 July 1757. Here is an account that I hope will be lively and at a human scale thanks to the great volume of memoirs and letters left by officers, both general and regimental, from the cavalry and infantry. Having left their garrisons four months earlier, the French army came to battle at the gates of Hanover after travelling more than 600 kilometres through Austrian and German lands.

Olivier Lapray

---

4   Comte Turpin de Crissé, *Commentaires sur les mémoires de Montecuculi* (Paris: Lacombe et Lejay, 1769), Vol.I, p.335.
5   Charles de Gaulle, *La France et son armée* (Paris: Plon, 1938).

1

The French Army in 1757

From 1748 to 1756, France lived in unprecedented prosperity, in an enormous expansion of intellectual and sensual pleasures … and when the war had to pull it out of this idleness of peace, the army, which still believed itself to be an army, suddenly found itself weakened at all levels of the hierarchy.[1]

The French army of 1757 had barely changed from the end of the reign of Louis XIV. It retained the same uses and abuses but unfortunately the latter had multiplied. Gambling, the luxuries of the table and its trappings made terrifying progress, and time was wasted with frivolous occupations. Apart from a few young talents such as the Comte de Gisors, son of *Maréchal* de Belle-Isle, the princes of the blood and higher cadres were not up to their task. Departing for war as if they were parading through the countryside, they were followed by a plethora of sedans, coaches, and personnel who slowed the army's progress. Senior roles were the prerogative of privileged families. Many *colonels* lacked any of the qualities necessary to be a good regimental commander. The camps set up on the Meuse, Moselle and Saar rivers in 1727 were nothing but pleasure grounds.

After the Austrian War of Succession, the government attempted to limit abuses and established new camps in peacetime where troops should be instructed and practice manoeuvres. The camps of *Lieutenant-général* Chevert in 1753 and 1755 were among the first to finally fulfil this role and significantly improved the firing capabilities of the armies which would change the face of future battles.

French infantry regiments were usually composed of four battalions. Regiments created more recently only had two, and some only one. Each battalion was divided into 17 companies including one of grenadiers and 16 of fusiliers for a theoretical strength of 685 men, excluding officers, per battalion.[2] The musket could fire several rounds per minute and thus stop a

---

1   Charles Pierre Victor, Comte Pajol, *Les guerres sous Louis XV* (Paris: Firmin-Didot, 1885), Vol.IV, p.52.
2   After a month of camps and marches in Westphalia, *Maréchal* d'Estrées counted his battalions at only 575 men apiece: letter to the minister, 2 July 1757.

HASTENBECK 1757

French infantrymen circa 1757. Unsigned drawing possibly by Duplessis-Bertaux or Eisen. (Anne S.K. Brown Collection)

charge at the last moment with fire against bladed weapons – the cavalry sabre or infantry bayonet. A small calibre cannon, called a *suédoise* [Swedish], was allocated to each battalion. Loaded with grapeshot, it increased the fire zone around the infantry.

The battalions supplied *piquets* of 50 men, three per company to spread the burden evenly. In war, these *piquets* were also used as detachments and so limited the impact of losses in the event of a disaster, as each *capitaine* who commanded a company was financially responsible for their own unit. The organization of the *piquet* was pernicious due to its major drawbacks in command and cohesion of fire, as explained by *Capitaine* Mercoyrol de Beaulieu of the Régiment de Picardie to his *colonel* on 25 July 1757, on the eve of the Battle of Hastenbeck:

> The Picardie brigade, under arms and in line, awaited the Navarre brigade, both were charged with the attack operation that day. It took *Général* Chevert's fancy to order that this brigade be arranged by *picquets* of fifty men, as was customary and still is, formed of three men per company … This proposal was found to be most remarkable, and there was not a *capitaine* who did not say to himself: Today I will fight with only three men of my company out of fifty, all the others will be unknown to me and to them, I will be unknown too; there will be no confidence on either side; I will be deprived of setting a good example to the soldiers whom I have tried to train well during seven years of toil; deprived of appointing such and such who I know to be full of courage, to watch over the conduct of such and such who had only been with the colours for four months, and others a year before as recruits; before my eyes I no longer have soldiers from the village, town, or countryside where I live! Add to all the unpleasant reflections that each capitaine made of such an order those which must have churned through the heads of each soldier, who would find himself with forty-seven companions from different companies, most of whom only knew each other by the uniform; moreover, there was not an officer who had served under the genius of the late *Maréchal* de Saxe, the present war emphasising the weight of his loss, who did not view the reputation of the Picardie Brigade compromised by the orders of General Chevert.

> M. de Bréhant, one of the brave *colonels* of the army and who commanded the regiment, was on the right with M. de Chevert.[3] Observing the consternation this order caused, he left the *Général* and came to see what was going on. I was a *peloton* [platoon] leader, with the Comte de Blou as my deputy, an officer from the Vivarais region like me, who is now *lieutenant-colonel* of the Régiment de Piedmont.[4]

3　Marie-Jacques, Marquis de Bréhant and Viscount of Lisle (1713-1764). *Lieutenant* of the Nicolay-Dragons in 1724, promoted to *brigadier* in 1748 and *colonel* of Picardie Regiment from 1749. He became *inspecteur général de infanterie* in 1760, *maréchal de camp* (major general) in 1761 and took part in all the campaigns from 1734 to 1761, in Germany, Flanders and Italy.

4　Jean-Louis de Blou de Chadenac (1737-1793), *lieutenant* of the Régiment de Picardie in 1746, *capitaine* by 1755. He became *lieutenant-colonel* of the Regiment de Troyes in 1771, then of Piedmont in 1776. During the Revolution became *colonel* of the 51e then 3e Régiment

I was one of the first to see M. de Bréhant come up to us. This officer was a friend and a certain confidence in me, acquired by my attention to think like him, by my zeal in carrying out his orders in peace time and my ardent desire to do the same during the war, continuing good proposals on all of the King's interests.

I advanced and said to him: "The formation M. de Chevert wants to give to your regiment is generally frowned upon by everyone; we all know that this order is taken in the trenches for reasons contrary to the good of the service". (This was done to prevent a company, which belonged to the *capitaine*, from suffering too much, for this crushed *compagnie* would ruin its *capitaine*). "But today, with this formation of *picquets*, after seven years of peace, when at least two-thirds of the soldiers are new and have only seen gunpowder burning during exercises in peace time, you must expect their honour will be compromised. This first French phalanx will perhaps make its first mistake today; the *colonel* will be killed, and with him fifty or sixty officers, but the blood of these brave men will not be enough to wash away the stain; it will last as long as the monarchy. You are the leader and your honour is first".

At the same time, M. de Bréhant was surrounded by forty officers who spoke unanimously with knowledge of war. The good, honest and brave M. de Bréhant had spent his summers with us; for seven years we had been preparing ourselves for war with him, in our conversations and our promenades. This was why we could take the liberty of telling him our opinion. He agreed with us and re-joined M. de Chevert to tell him how the regiment was hard against the formation he ordered. M. de Chevert's reply was not very consistent; he alleged that, when he wished fifty or a hundred men of the regiment to march, he would be sure of the correct composition by using one or two *piquets*.

M. de Bréhant was met again when, out of impatience, our *peloton* joined by several other officers, approached him. He informed us of the general's response, to which we unanimously replied, to tell the *général* that when he needed fifty or a hundred men, to order one or two companies to march and that although they were reduced to thirty men under arms by the detached or sick, we all agreed to draw the service of fifty men. M. de Bréhant gave in to our wishes.[5]

When fighting together in pitched battle, battalions were formed in line of four ranks, however, preserving the width of the line was considered very important and so the ranks were quickly reduced to three after any serious action. Because of this, attacking flanking manoeuvres were significant, especially if battalions were not trained to quickly change their order of battle. France was only just beginning to formalise and develop regulations for infantry manoeuvres. Attack columns were widely used. Soldiers were

---

d'Infanterie in 1791, *général de brigade* in 1792 and *général de division* in 1793. He was killed by a bomb that fell in the courtyard of the headquarters in Mainz on June 27, 1793.

5 Marquis de Vogüé & Auguste Le Sourd, *Campagnes de Jacques de Mercoyrol de Beaulieu, captain au regiment de Picardie (1743-1763)* (Renouard: Society of the History of France, 1915), p.116-120. Jacques de Mercoyrol de Beaulieu (1725-1817), enlisted at seventeen in the Régiment de Picardie where his uncle was *capitaine*. He was made *lieutenant* in 1743, *capitaine* in 1749, and would become *major* of the regiment in 1760. He left the regiment to become a *brigadier* in 1780 and retired as a *maréchel de camp* in 1784. The account of his campaigns was written in 1788.

deployed above five deep, columns were formed to ensure the order and cohesion of the attack.

French infantry brigades were made up of several regiments. However, there was a peculiarity that regiments with four battalions were sometimes referred to as a brigade. Therefore, rather than referring to the Régiment de Picardie instead it would be called the Brigade de Picardie.[6]

Infantry brigades were formed alternately in line and column, and great use was made of the attacking column in battalions, sometimes flanked on either side by a deployed section or company. Column formation took place around the centre of the battalion which made complex evolutions on the battlefield as the *pelotons* first had to double up and then those on the wings would line up behind the centre.

The Prussian army proceeded in oblique order, achieved by battalions passing from line, facing the enemy, to column to moving obliquely to one of its wings which they then attacked in line after making a quarter turn to face them. However, unless it was concealed from the enemies' sight, this manoeuvre required a risky flank march. The manoeuvre was made simpler with platoons forming one after the other, behind the base platoon.

There were numerous French light troops. They fought in front of the columns in a dispersed manner, taking advantage of the difficult positions to hold up an enemy, sometimes in great in number. However, the intensive use of small detachments imposed a great dispersion of skirmishers so that it was that infantry battalions were also used for small operations and outpost combats.

A large detachment of several battalions, with its firepower and a well-supported position, could receive the attack of an enemy army. As such, commanders-in-chief begin to detach their army vanguard to such good positions. Divisions of combined arms also began to be formed around this time, not only for manoeuvre but also in camps and siege operations. Usually though, armies remained massed together, rarely exceeding 60,000 men. The proportions of artillery and cavalry were important and in the Prussian army reached one cannon for every 300 infantry and one cavalryman for every three infantrymen.

As for the French cavalry, its regiments consisted mainly of two squadrons [*escadrons*] of four companies of 40 troopers, making a theoretical complete complement of 328 men per regiment.[7] Regiments of dragoons and hussars were organised with four squadrons of two companies of 75 men each, so were almost double strength of the other cavalry. In the field, cavalry employed patrols of four to six men under the orders of a non-commissioned officer for scouting the enemy or troops of 20-30 cavalrymen under the orders of a *lieutenant* or a *cornet* as guards. The most frequent detachment for outposts and large guards was a troop of 50 cavalrymen picked from all the companies of the regiment. The only improvements to uniformity in the

---

6   For clarity on this point, see the appendices detailing the composition of the French army during this campaign.

7   After crossing the Rhine at Weser, there were only 280 mounted men per regiment under arms in the French army in Westphalia (camp at Beilfeld, 1 July 1757).

HASTENBECK 1757

Gunner (right) and *Ouvrier* (left) of the Corps Royal de l'artillerie et du genie. (NYPL Vinkhuijzen Collection)

cavalry that had been made since the beginning of the century was their manoeuvres. They generally formed in two ranks, a third having a special role, to provide skirmishers for example. Organisation and tactics had not improved in comparison to Prussia, which over the same period had evolved into what can be regarded as the first modern cavalry regulations. 'But more serious and more inexcusable was the scant regard made for the tactical principles of Drummond de Melfort, which the routine and inertia of the senior military figures had [reduced] to the lethargy and formalism of the ordinance of 1755'.[8]

In 1755 the artillery was merged with the engineers into a single Corps Royal de l'artillerie et du génie which consisted of a staff of 31 officers, six companies of miners, six companies of *ouvriers* [workers], 300 engineers, and six artillery battalions. Each battalion had 16 companies: two of sappers, nine of gunners, and five of bombardiers. The 50-man artillery companies served medium-calibre guns from the Army Reserve Park independently of the small-calibre guns used by the infantry regiments. Indeed, 'these 4pdrs, attached to the regiment at the rate of one per battalion, were served by soldiers of the said battalions at the rate of sixteen men for each of them, who were perfectly instructed to aim and fire them with the perfect speed and manoeuvre them with all the formations a regiment can make'.[9]

Ultimately one could reasonably say that *Maréchal* d'Estrées would take on the campaign of 1757 in Westphalia at the head of a 'large army but one that was not suited to pursue the war with energy'.[10]

---

8   E. Desbriére & M. Sautai, *La cavalerie de 1740 à 1789* (Paris: Berger-Levrault, 1906), p.22.
9   Vogüé & Sourd, *Campagnes de Mercoyrol de Beaulieu*, p.122.
10 Friedrich August de Retzow, *Nouveaux mémoires historiques sur la guerre de Sept ans* (Paris: Treuttel et Würtz, 1803), Vol.I, p.214. Friedrich August de Retzow (1729-1812) had been a captain in Prussian service and was son of General Wolf Friedrich de Retzow (1699-1758), who commanded the regiment that he served in as adjutant-major in 1757. He retired after the death of his father in 1758 and took part in the 1760 campaign as aide-de-camp to the King of Prussia.

2

The Beginning of the Seven Years War

So began the Seven Years War which was not as glorious for our armies as it could have been; nevertheless, it was without doubt the most memorable part of Louis XV's reign. It served as a lesson and example for the troops of the European powers, and educated a large number of good officers.[1]

After the War of the Austrian Succession when the French and the Prussians had fought the Austrians eight years earlier, a new conflict, emblematic of Franco-British rivalry, broke out in Canada over what Voltaire would call 'a few acres of snow'. This Seven Years War overturned the alliances of Europe. It would set France, Russia, Sweden, and Austria against Great Britain and Prussia from 1756 to 1763.

For France, the war began successfully in Canada, where the Marquis de Montcalm, sent with 4,500 men, defeated the English in several battles, and in Europe, where the Duc de Richelieu stormed Port-Mahon and captured the island of Menorca after a victory over the English fleet. The alliance with Maria Theresa, Empress of Austria and Queen of Hungary, allowed the King of France to confront England without fearing the opening of a second front in Europe. In the autumn of 1756, preparations were made for the next year's campaign, which seemed assured to lead to peace. There was even a rumour that an invasion into Great Britain was being prepared, so that Hanoverian and Hessian troops were called to reinforce the British Isles.

However, Frederick II of Prussia took the initiative. He made a pre-emptive thrust towards an attack he expected from the Austro-Russian armies, and left his borders. On 29 August 1756, without a declaration of war, he invaded the Electorate of Saxony at the head of an army of 64,000 men and threatened Bohemia. Dresden was taken. The elector, who was also King of Poland, was allowed to withdraw to Poland but his defeated army was disarmed; the Saxons were incorporated into the Prussian army.

---

1   Pajol, *Les guerres sous Louis XV*, Vol.IV, p.52.

After suffering heavy casualties during an incursion into Bohemia, Frederick retreated to establish winter quarters in Saxony and Silesia.

Without losing sight of maritime and colonial interests, French priorities began to shift in favour of operations in Europe. Touched by an affront to his family and out of respect for his commitments to Austria, Louis XV was no longer opposed to campaigning in Germany.[2] French aims naturally focused on the English possessions in Hanover. During the winter, the Comte d'Estrées was sent to Vienna to plan for the next campaign. Louis Charles César Le Tellier, Comte d'Estrées (1695-1771) had been *inspecteur-général de cavalrie* and distinguished himself under *Maréchal* de Saxe at the Battle of Fontenoy in 1745.

On 14 January 1757, an agreement was reached. The Austrian Netherlands were to be protected to force Holland to maintain its promised neutrality; the Prussian districts bordering the Rhine would be seized, in particular Wesel and Gelderland, to force the Landgrave of Hesse-Cassel to abandon the English cause; the French would then to cross the Weser and move on to the Elbe to threaten Prussia. The Rhineland possessions of Frederick II would be returned to Austria while the lands of Hanover would be occupied by France, particularly the fortress of Hameln which would be garrisoned. In Versailles, the route marches were finalised as the Comte d'Estreés worked to smooth out the difficulties of passage through the Netherlands and states of the Austrian Empire. The comte's mission finally ended with an arrangement regarding heavy artillery and siege expenses as well as decisions of service in the combined armies.

On his return from Vienna, the Comte d'Estrées was named *général-en-chef* of the army assembled on the lower Rhine. His abilities were held in high opinion having made his reputation serving under the de Saxe who had employed him on numerous occasions, notably at Fontenoy. On 24 February, the King appointed him *Maréchal de France* commanding the auxiliary army destined to enter Westphalia and move on Hanover. This army was

Louis Charles César Le Tellier, Comte d'Estrées. (Public Domain)

---

2   Louis XV had married his eldest son to Marie-Josèphe of Saxony, daughter of the Elector of Saxony and King of Poland. This marriage produced the future Louis XVI, born two years earlier.

considered to the finest seen in a long time. The Comte de Maillebois was appointed *maréchal général de logis* [chief of staff] and M. de Lucé as *intendant*.³ The Duc d'Orléans, first prince of the blood, was appointed as second in command and would deputize for the *Maréchal* in case of absence or illness.

On 1 May 1757 the second Treaty of Versailles was signed which agreed that France would participate in military operations until Austria had reconquered Silesia. In return France would gain parts of the Austrian Netherlands: the Chimay and Beaumont regions of Belgium and the towns of Mons, Ypres, Furnes as well as the ports of Ostende and Nieuport. It was time to go on the offensive. Louis XV agreed to mobilise 100,000 men in Germany, to pay 12 million guilders a year to Austria and to finance half of the subsidies allocated to Saxony and Sweden.

King George II of Great Britain was also the Elector of Hanover; it was said of him that:

> [H]is preferences and his German prejudices were notorious. He was known to be more concerned with the fate of his country of Hanover than that of Great Britain. His dearest desire was to spare the Electorate from the scourge of war. He thought this goal could be achieved by dealing with the King of Prussia, despite his lack of taste for his relative.⁴

He had hoped to obtain the neutrality of Hanover from Austria so as not to engage England in a continental war which alarmed his Parliament. However at the end of April, faced with conditions posed by the Empress that he deemed unacceptable, George II resolved to prevent the threat. He decided on raising an Army of Observation on the Weser composed of Hanoverian and Hessian troops, commanded by his third son, the Duke of Cumberland.

On the Prussian side Frederick II decided to strike a blow before the enemy armies could join together. He hoped to take advantage of the four-month head start he had on the Russian army on account of them having to wait to emerge from the frosts. During the first part of 1757, he faced the Austrian armies alone. The Prussian army was larger, made up of old, disciplined troops who were better trained in manoeuvres because the King had long organized his country like a vast military camp. The subsidies he received from Britain had also given him the means to raise soldiers and officers throughout Germany. Frederick II therefore chose to invade Bohemia and besiege Prague which he had failed to do the year before. 'There, as in a large

---

3   Yves-Marie Desmarets, Comte de Maillebois, born in 1715, son of the *maréchal* of the same name. Promoted *lieutenant-général* in 1748, he had been *inspecteur général l'infanterie* and *maître de la garde-robe du roi*. In 1758 he spread a libel insulting *Maréchal* d'Estreés about the battle of Hastenbeck and was brought before a court-martial which sentenced him to prison. He was released after a stay in the citadel of Doullens but would remain in disgrace until the end of his days. He died in emigration at Liège, in 1791, in a hurried counter-revolution project.

4   Richard Waddington, *La guerre de Sept ans: histoire diplomatique et militaire – Les débuts* (Paris: Firmin-Didot, 1899), p.192.

entrenched camp, he would have protected Saxony and Silesia, containing Austria and the Empire'.[5]

The French army of *Maréchal* d'Estrées, which was preparing to cross the Rhine 'was intended to open the war, which the court of Versailles had resolved to bring to the continent … because they saw the impossibility of standing up to the English at sea, they flattered themselves to draw them from operations in the two Indies, by invading the Electorate of Hanover'.[6]

---

5 Napoleon I, *Précis dés guerres de Frédéric II, commentaires sur la guerre de Sept ans* (Réèdition: Amazon, 2018), p.27.
6 De Retzow, *Nouveaux mémoires*, p.213.

3

Assembly on the Rhine

> *The army continued its march had arrived at Wesel, where a bridge of boats had been constructed over the Rhine where it crossed. There was a gathering of all the armies.*[1]

The Prince de Soubise had been appointed the provisional commander of an army of 24,000 men on 1 January 1757 which the court of Versailles had agreed to supply to the Queen of Hungary. On 25 February, the Prince received his instructions as well as new powers to take command of a separate reserve body whose objective was, depending on circumstances, to operate in concert with the Austrian army in Bohemia or to stand by to reunite with the auxiliary army of *Maréchal* d'Estrées. While awaiting the *Maréchal*, the Prince de Soubise prepared the establishment of the troops on the lower Rhine with the Comte de Maillebois. Pending the outcome of negotiations on the neutrality of the Electorate of Hanover, 53,000 men would leave Düsseldorf to act against the Rhine possessions of the King of Prussia, starting with the capture of Geldern and Wesel, in the Duchy of Cleves.

An optimistic *Maréchal* de Belle-Isle, the King's minister of war, wrote to *Maréchal* d'Estrées 'I tried to foresee everything with the same attention as if I had command of the army myself'.[2] Necessary requisitions were sent to the German princes whose territories had to be crossed. The directions of the route marches were fixed, the stores of food and hospitals arranged, the passports of the Empress dispatched, and the French and Imperial commissioners sent to the crossing points with all the necessary supplies for the troops. Letters of service were addressed to generals and staff officers which ordered them to report for duty by 25 April. The infantry *colonels* and cavalry *mestre-de-camps* ordered their officers to prepare their men.

March was devoted readying provisions for the route. The first half of the army was to leave its garrisons later in the month, detaching the agreed 53,000 men in Düsseldorf between 25 and 30 April. The second half of the army would leave a little later for the Rhine and the rear guard would regroup

---

1   Vogüé & Sourd, *Campagnes de Mercoyrol de Beaulieu*, p. 110.
2   Belle-Isle to d'Estrées, 2 February 1757 in Waddington, *La guerre de Sept ans*, p.104.

with it around 15 May. The Siege of Wesel was due to begin around 10 May. A special agreement was established for the occupation of Düsseldorf. Despite various treaties made to ensure supplies, difficulties were already emerging getting stores on the left bank of the Rhine and the supply of fodder for the horses. The services of the Parisian intendant had preferred to begin making impositions on the magistrates of the country and so hindered direct purchases from individuals, whose demands and selfishness caused the army commissioners to pay exaggerated prices.

The first to march towards the lower Rhine were four squadrons and 12 battalions which went from Toul, Metz, Thionville, Sarrelouis or Phalsbourg sur Neuss and Linnich, between Aix-la-Chapelle and Düsseldorf.[3] The Volontaires Royaux and Régiment de Lameth Cavalerie were the first to leave. Columns left Valenciennes, Lille, and Maubeuge to reassemble between the Meuse and the lower Rhine. The regiments marched in stages of 10-20 kilometres with one rest day out of five. Each soldier received a ration of seven quarters of bread and three quarters of meat and had the right to housing, fire, and light free of charge. Bread was made with a two-thirds wheat and one-third of rye ratio at a cost of two *sols* six *deniers* and the price of meat was fixed at three or four *sols* per pound. Each battalion had a four-wheeled cart to transport tents and haversacks.

The column that marched towards the Rhine was kept in good condition because the spirited soldiers kept the most exact discipline despite the bad weather, logistical difficulties and fatigue. The Comte de Gisors, *colonel* of the Régiment de Champagne, wrote to his father the *Maréchal* de Belle-Isle:

> We did not leave a man behind … the cheerfulness and goodwill of the soldiers are great, but they are young people who must be taken care of so that their strength is maintained until the end of the campaign … You know that in these parts how many jurisdictions are divided; half of a village depends on one, the other half on another. A company has its accommodation ticket for such a village where there are two or three different mayors; if it is addressed to one rather than the other, he will dismiss it without further explanation. We have had some who travelled two leagues around a city before finding shelter; and dispersed as they are, it will be a great proof of our discipline if no disorder occurs.[4]

As the threat of French invasion of Britain subsided, the last Hanoverian troops to leave England arrived at the lower Elbe on 2 March. The Hanoverian army was assembling from Werden up to Nienburg on the Weser and from Rodenberg to Hameln, awaiting the arrival of contingents from Brunswick, Hesse and Saxe-Gotha. When complete it was estimated that this army, reinforced by the Prussian garrison of Wesel and a few other troops from Magdeburg, would total 50,000 men. The Prussians, whose emissaries bought

---

3   Four squadrons of the Lameth cavalry, 12 battalions of the Volontaires Royaux and the regiments of Champagne, Nassau-Saarbruck, Royal Bavière, Dauphine, Royal-Pologne, Royal-Suédois, and Saint-Germain.

4   Gisors to Belle-Isle, Sierck 3 April 1757 and Saarbourg 6 April 1757 in Waddington, *La guerre de Sept ans*, pp.387-388.

HASTENBECK 1757

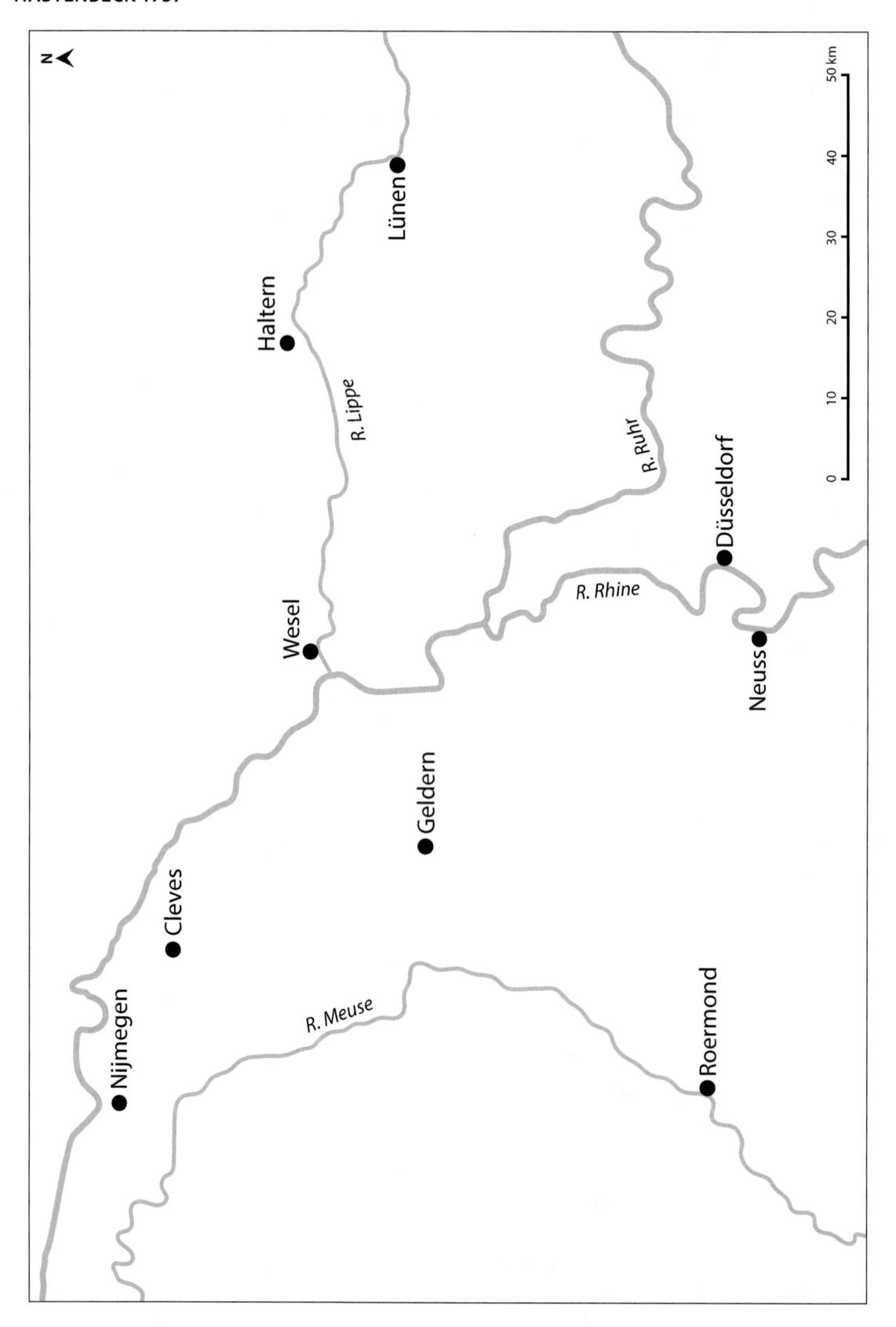

grain and fodder in Upper Franconia and the Upper Main, still held Wesel, 'a prodigiously fortified place which, together with its position at the confluence of the Rhine and the Lippe, made it a formidable position'.[5] Frederick II had proposed to make it a stronghold and establish the Hanoverian army behind the Lippe so as to guard Westphalia but had had to give up the defence of his territory in Westphalia and prepare to withdraw the Wesel garrison, sending 6,000 men to the Duke of Cumberland.

> I must say here that Wesel is a large and beautiful city, well-fortified, with an infinity of works and a citadel whose right rests on the right bank of the Rhine which runs along the entire length of the city. The King of Prussia … saw that leaving a garrison of at least 10,000 men for the defence, with all kinds of munitions, a large number of artillery and a large quantity of food, he would only stop the French army for two months, of which he knew the quick and lively manner of siege and capture. He skilfully judged that these two months which Wesel would apparently be the advantageous halting of the French army, would in fact produce an acceleration of the French advance as for the duration of the siege, stores and supplies could be established to carry us forward with speed; also that the French army would gain by being toughened by this siege … [and] that moreover it would be a stain on his honour of arms.[6]

On 15 March the Prussian garrison began the evacuation of Wesel. On the 24th, it completed its withdrawal to Lippstadt after destroying part of the works on the Lippe and Rhine side. This Pyrrhic success did not allow operations to advance as we have seen that 'the French troops would be ready to cross the Rhine sooner than the preparations made to receive them and provide for their subsistence'.[7]

The Prince de Soubise, the acting commander, left Paris on 21 March, arrived in Brussels on the 24th, Tongres on the 26th, Maaseik on the 27th and Roermond on the 28th.[8] Learning of the evacuation of Wesel, assumed to be under siege, he sent out 100 men of the Austrian Regimnet de Ligne and 400 Chasseurs de Fischer from Roermond to Prussian Guelders and from the Rhine to Cleves, Rees, and Büderich to stop the evacuating boats from sailing up the river. The Prince worked with the Comtes de Maillebois and Saint-Germain to establish the 24 battalions and four squadrons he commanded.[9] The country between the Meuse and the Rhine was inspected around Heinsberg and Wassenberg, 20 kilometres south-east of Roermond.

---

5   Antoine Rigobert Mopinot de la Chapotte, *Sous Louis le Bien-Aimé: correspondence amoureuse et militaire d'un officier pendant la guerre de Sept-ans (1743-1763)* (Paris: Calmann-Lévy, 1905), p.23. Chapotte was a *capitaine* in the Régiment de Dauphin Cavalerie at this time.
6   Vogüé & Sourd, *Campagnes de Mercoyrol de Beaulieu*, p.111.
7   Duc de Luynes, *Mémoires du duc de Luynes sur la Cour de Louis XV* (Paris: Firmin-Didot, 1864), Vol.XV, p.249. Note from October 1756.
8   The Comte de Maillebois followed on 26 February, then the Comtes de Saint-Germain and Lorges on the 27th and then La Couronne on the 28th of March. *Gazette*, no. 15 du 9 avril 1757.
9   Claude Louis Robert, Comte de Saint-Germain (1707-1778) had served in the armies of the German palatine, Austria and Bavaria. He was appointed *lieutenant-général* in the service of

Officers reconnoitred positions along the left bank of the Rhine from Neuss in the south, to Cleves in the north, to facilitate crossing the river when the time came. Three of the four Austrian battalions from Roermond were dispatched to the Duchy of Cleves under the orders of the Comte de Dombasle, an officer of French origin and *Generalmajor* in the Austrian army, followed by the first columns already announced at Linnich, north of Aix-la-Chapelle, and Neuss.[10] The requested reconnaissance on Geldern reported that they were working on canal locks and flooding.

On the 3 April, the Régiment de Belzunce arrived in Neuss where the Prince de Soubise established his headquarters on the same day. He left the Comte de Lorges, *lieutenant-général*, in command of the force lodged in Cleves and the Marquis de Saint-Chamans, *maréchal de camp*, the troops in front of Geldern.[11] Two days later, the Prince went to Düsseldorf while the Comte de Chabo, commanding the brigade of Volontaires Royaux and Chasseurs de Fischer, left with a detachment to secure any ammunition that the Prussians might have left in Wesel and prepare it to receive a French and Austrian garrison.[12] Another reconnaissance by the Volontaires Royaux and Chasseurs de Fischer pushed east of Wesel, on the Lippe, to prevent any grain and tax payments heading to the King of Prussia.

The plan drawn up on 3 April in Versailles with *Maréchal* d'Estrées did not foresee leaving Münster before 20 May. The Comte de Maillebois, who was with the army, was even more certain that 'the head of the troops will not arrive at a crossing of the Rhine before 12 April … Only 22 battalions can be put together by the 14th, crossing and having to be reinforced successively … We will be very happy if we can pass Münster before June 1st. I wish it if it is the intention of the *Maréchal*, but I dare not hope for it'.[13]

On 6 April the Comte de Dombasle entered Cleves with three Austrian battalions from the former Roermond garrison. A commissioner immediately came to take possession of the city in the name of the Queen of Hungary. On 8 April, two battalions of the Régiment de Belzunce and two of Austrians, from Cleves, made their entry into Wesel with the Comte de Saint-Germain, *lieutenant-général*, commanding. At the same time, it was discovered that the Hanoverian troops would take up their quarters along the Weser and that the 3,000 Prussians that had left Wesel continued their retreat northward from

---

France in 1748 and would become a field marshal of Denmark in 1762 and minister of war for Louis XVI from 1775 to 1777.

10   The four Austrian battalions were from the regiments of Saxe-Gotha, de Ligne, Los-Rios and Arberg.

11   Guy Louis de Durfort de Lorges (1714-1775), was brother of the Duc de Randan. He was made *maréchal de camp* in 1745, *lieutenant-général* in 1748 and Duc de Lorges in 1759.

12   Louis Charles de Chabo de la Serre, Comte de Chabo (1715-1780) commanded the Régiment des Volontaires Royaux and was a *brigadier* from 1748. He was made *maréchal de camp* in 1758 and *lieutenant-général* in 1762. He was the brother of Antoine, chevalier de Chabo (1716-1777) who was also *général des logis de la cavalrie de l'armée* for the *Maréchal* d'Estrées, became *maréchal de camp de cavalerie* in 1761, and wrote the tactical work, *l'Abrégé des commentaires de M. de Folard*.

13   'Observations du comte de Maillebois sur e plan d'opérations', 6 April 1757 in Waddington, *La guerre de Sept ans*, p.389.

ASSEMBLY ON THE RHINE

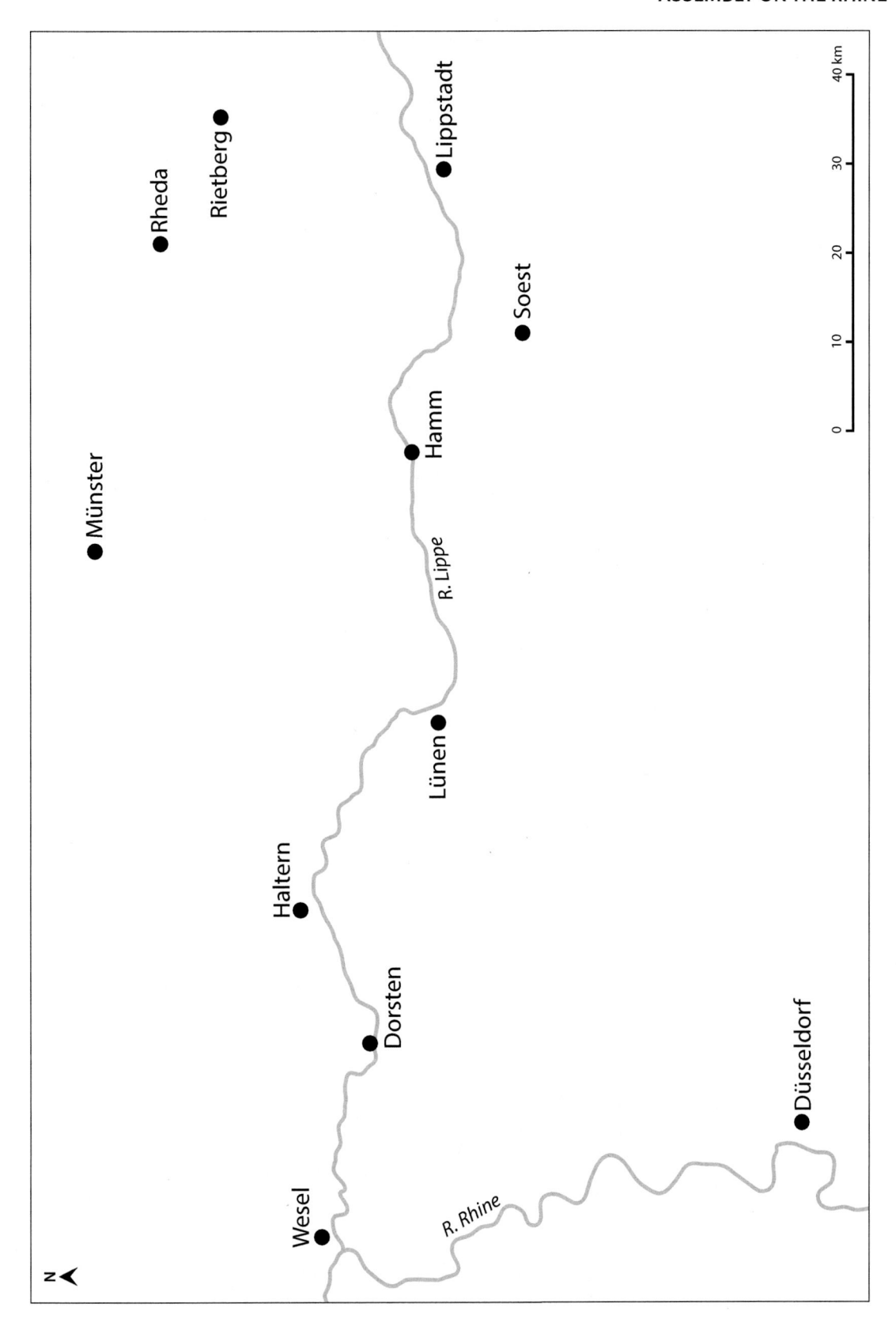

Lippstadt to Rietberg and on to Bielefeld, in the County of Ravensberg, a Prussian possession.

During this time the four battalions of the Franco-Austrian garrison of Wesel was reinforced by the other two battalions of the Régiment de Belzunce on the 10th and one of the two battalions of the Swiss Régiment de Reding, in the service of the King of France, on the 11th. The other regiments and the large artillery and engineer contingent continued to move along the Rhine. On the 7 April the *Gazette* reported that the day before there had arrived in Brussels:

> [S]ixty copper pontoons, a large quantity of powder and cannonballs and other artillery ammunition, with 500 horses for pulling cannons and mortars.[14] 500 more horses will arrive today for the same purpose. The guns and mortars were loaded from Douai sur la Scarpe to be transported by the Sambre and Meuse rivers to Liège, from where the aforementioned 1,000 horses will take them to the camp of the French army. The troops of this army, which passed through this town last week to go to Stockem, are two battalions of the Régiment d'Aquitaine, two of the Régiment de Provence, four of the Régiment de Picardie, one battalion [each] of the Régiment de Périgord and de Foix. Two squadrons of the Régiment de Cavalerie de Saluces arrived on the 4th. The La Motte artillery company arrived on the 3rd. A second column of French troops is expected later this month, comprising 16 infantry battalions, 12 squadrons of cavalry and 16 squadrons of dragoons. The battalions are four of the Grenadiers Royaux, four of Grenadiers de France, the Régiment du Roi and four from the Régiment de Navarre. The cavalry squadrons are two from Dauphin, two from Dauphin-Étranger, two from the la Reine, two from Royal-Piémont, two from Lénoncourt and two from Charost. The dragoon squadrons are four from the Colonel-Général, four from the Mestre de Camp-Général, four from Orléans and four from Harcourt.[15]

The Prince de Soubise sent a detachment of 2,500 men under the orders of the Comte de Maillebois, *lieutenant-général*, and the Marquis de Crillon, *maréchal de camp*, to go towards the Lippe and approach the rich town of Münster, which was intimidated by the proximity of the Prussians. The Comte was to make contact with the authorities there in order to get a better intelligence of the country. He went eastward along the Lippe on 10 April with his detachment and spent the night in Dorsten at the gates of the diocese of Münster. The next day, he advanced to Haltern on the Lippe then moved obliquely northeast towards Dülmen over the next two days. He left the Marquis at Dülmen with the main body of the detachment and took just 20 Volontaires Royaux and 100 of Chasseurs de Fischer to Bulderen. This was four leagues from Münster, whose authorities wished to maintain their neutrality while awaiting instructions from the Elector of Cologne. The Elector seemed rather well disposed to the French, but his subjects were not. 'Send men to camp at Dorsten on the Lippe and let them torch all the

---

14 Translator's note: Copper-bottomed pontoons (*ponton de cuivre*) was the name given to craft used to transport troops over rivers as floating bridges.
15 'De Bruxelles, le 7 avril 1757', *Gazette*, nombre 16 du 16 avril 1757.

possessions located in the States of the King of Prussia which belong to the ill-intentioned people of the city of Münster' wrote a French ambassador close to the Elector.[16]

The Comte de Maillebois, having conferred on the city of Münster's situation with one of the main members of the local regency and an *aide-maréchal-général* of the French army who resided there, returned to Haltern on the 13th then Wesel on the 14th, where the Prince de Soubise had established headquarters the same day. The Comte left his detachment in echelon on the Lippe under the orders of the Marquis de Crillon, having taken care to write a letter to the regency requesting access for the French troops to the country of Münster and to provide for the subsistence arrangements for the troops of the King in the grounds of the Bishop's Palace.

The Prince de Soubise received information of Prussian troops at Lippstadt which he assumed came with the intention of consuming the fodder that was still available between Lippe and Weser. In response he decided to send two Austrian battalions from Wesel to Schermbeck on the 15 April, 20 kilometres to the east, to be joined by Régiment de Reding the next day. On the 17th, 15 battalions crossed the Rhine to reinforce the vanguard. With the Marquis de Crillon and de Rougé, *maréchal de camp*, under his command, the Comte de Saint-Germain was ordered to advance to Haltern and Lünen on the Lippe with 10 battalions and four squadrons. With this manoeuvre, the Prince of Soubise intended to force the enemy to cross the Weser and ensure subsistence and places to billet soldiers beyond the Rhine for the beginning of the campaign.

The Duke of Cumberland had set out from Warwick on 9 April and arrived in Hanover on the morning of the 16th to take command of the Army of Observation which was due to assemble on the 25th at the borders of the Electorate. On 20 April, with the enemy still in Lippstadt, the Prince de Soubise decided to force them to withdraw by advancing a strong detachment. The Prince de Beauvau, *maréchal de camp*, marched on Münster with the six battalions of the Régiments de Vastan, Conti and La Couronne, with 100 artillerymen, 40 dragoons and 50 Chasseurs de Fischer, supported on the right by the Comte de Saint-Germain who was pushing up to Hamm with the Régiment de Belzunce on the 22nd and with detachments on both banks of the Lippe.[17]

The government of Münster initially refused to admit troops to the city so the Prince de Beauvau could not lodge there until 23 April. The same day, with the enemy still at Lippstadt, the Prince de Soubise sent a detachment of the Corps Royal de l'artillerie et du génie with six 12-pounders to the Comte de Saint-Germain to support an advance of eight battalions and two squadrons from the Rhine between the Lippe and the Ruhr. On the 25th, the Prince of Hesse, threatened with being cut off by the Comte de Saint-

---

16   Letter of 25 March 1757.
17   The Régiment de Belzunce (4 battalions) was at Hamm; Régiment de Reding (2 battalions) a little further forward at Ahlen and the Austrians (2 battalions) further north-east at Beckum with the Voluntaires Royaux furthest advanced at Stromberg towards Rheda above Lippstadt; the rest of the detachment was on the left bank of the Lippe.

Germain, decided to evacuate Lippstadt. He left the County of Rietberg after collecting taxes, but took only a single cannon from the castle due to a lack of horses to pull it, and retreated to the Weser. The Comte de Saint-Germain entered Lippstadt on the 26th. The town, situated in marshy terrain, was occupied by the four battalions of the Régiment de Belzunce while the rest of the troops were echeloned further back towards the south-west at Soest, Werl, Lünen and then Dortmund for the battalions arriving from the Rhine.

The army's bulletin for 3 May recorded:

> M. le Comte de Saint-Germain left on 16 April, having ten battalions and the Volontaires Royaux under his orders. By his manoeuvres he obliged the Prince of Hesse to abandon the town of Lippstadt … This position was taken by the Comte de Saint-Germain: in Lippstadt four battalions of Belzunce, the Volontaires Royaux covering the right at Erwitte, the Austrians on the right in the villages of Stirpe and Berenbrock; Reding-Suisse in the centre, at Horn and Schemerleke; Poitou, to the left, at Eickelborn, Benninghausen and Overhagen. All these villages border the Geisler stream. The rallying point is at Overhagen Castle. By this order, Lippstadt is very well supported; but if against all expectations he was forced back, M. le Comte de Saint-Germain has formulated a very good retreat to Hamm, where there are troops. Lippstadt is currently being accommodated; we make redoubts and flèches on the glacis to close the gap of the defences at the river.[18]

More than 80 boats descended the Rhine from Strasbourg, transporting pontoons and other large equipment but the advance of the army was delayed by the lack of fodder. As Soubise wrote, 'The only thing which we can be troubled; we will not lack bread, meat and oats, but hay is really scarce; it is necessary to have recourse to neighbouring countries and the transport is long'.[19] If the army had spent the two months thought needed to besiege Wesel, the army would have entered Westphalia in the hay season.

In the camps, *colonels* were engaged in the training and manoeuvring of soldiers to 'Apply to war the order sought to be established during peace'. The Comte de Gisors continued:

> My only talk with my *capitaines* is on the profession and the training of my *lieutenants*, divided into first and second class, as are my soldiers. And so in this campaign, I will be happy enough that they fire their muskets successfully, [but] I will give more credit to the minds that can give a young man a little enthusiasm for novelties ahead and keep quiet with stories of adventures in which, despite disorder, we succeed.[20]

---

18 'Bulletin de l'armée du bas Rhin du 3 mai' in Duc de Luynes, *Mémoires du duc de Luynes*, Vol. XVI, p.48.
19 Prince de Soubise to Marquis de Paulmy, Secretary of State for War, 27 April 1757 in Waddington, *La guerre de Sept ans*, p.390.
20 Gisors to Belle-Isle, 29 April 1757 in Camille Rousset, *Le comte de Gisors (1732-1758)* (Paris: Didier, 1868), p.163.

In Hanover, meanwhile:

> [S]everal obstacles delayed the march of the troops of the Electorate. Most of the regiments only left their quarters on the 20th of this month and the guards did not leave the capital until yesterday. Allied troops are also marching very slowly. Those of Brunswick are currently passing through the diocese of Hildesheim. It is believed, however, that part of the Observation Army will be assembled [by 30 April] and that the Duke of Cumberland will report to camp the following day … the hereditary Prince of Brunswick-Wolfenbüttel arrived here on [26 April]. The Count of Lippe-Buckebourg, who will command the regiment he has raised in the pay of this Electorate, is expected there shortly.[21]

On 27 April, the Prince de Soubise handed over command of the troops to *Maréchal* d'Estrées, who had just reached the army. In return, he received the leadership of the reserve corps, made up of 16 battalions and 24 squadrons partly assembled under the orders of the Comte de Saint-Germain, who would continue to operate in the vanguard autonomously but subordinate to the *Maréchal*.

---

21   'De Hanovre, le 28 avril 1757', *Gazette*, no. 20, 14 mai 1757.

4

Between the Rhine and the Lippe

D'Estrées took on a very difficult role. He had enemies in his army far more formidable than those who awaited him beyond the Rhine; and the particular orders of the court already put enough obstacles the enterprise.[1]

Maréchal d'Estrées had gone to Versailles to communicate the plans made in Vienna. He took leave of the King on 19 April and left for the army on the 20th with his instructions. He spent the night of the 26th at the Neuss camp, and reviewed the Régiment de Champagne before leaving, arriving at Wesel on the 27th, around 4:00 p.m. The location plan of the troops was given to him on his arrival which found more advanced than he hoped: 50 battalions and 20 squadrons were quartered between the Meuse and the Rhine, 34 battalions and 16 squadrons had been placed beyond the Rhine on the Lippe, in Münster, and in the Duchy of Berg while the rest continue to arrive little by little. Immediately informed of the shortage in fodder, he ordered all the officers to send surplus of their entourage back to France and set an example himself.

Only a third of the infantry and an eighth of the cavalry crossed the Rhine, but the army entrusted to *Maréchal* d'Estrées would eventually number more than 110 infantry battalions, 140 cavalry squadrons and 90 field pieces, without counting the light artillery attached to the infantry (one gun per battalion). Compared to the total number of Royal troops – 236 battalions and 222 squadrons – this was a considerable army of about 95,000 men (see the order of battle in Appendix 1).

'A considerable army' was also the view of the Duc de Luynes in February 1757 when he compared the available king's troops:

> The King's has … 236 battalions of regular troops; there are 11 in Mahon, 3 departed with M. de Lally for India, 8 bound for Corsica with M. de Castries, 6 to be sent

---

1 De Retzow, *Nouveaux mémoires*, Vol.I, p.214.

BETWEEN THE RHINE AND THE LIPPE

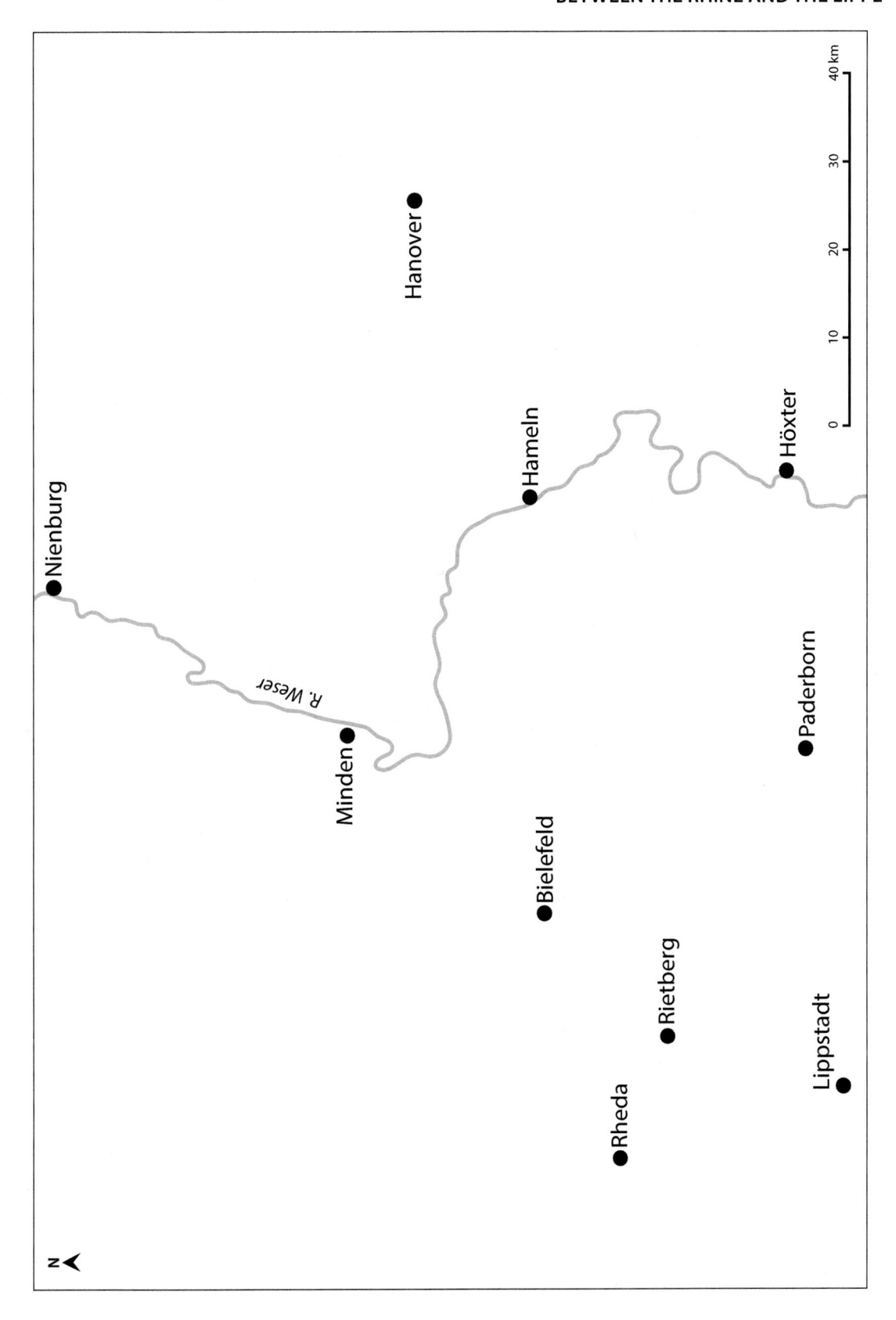

to Canada with M. de Montcalm; so there are [a total of] 28 employed at different destinations; leaving 208. These battalions are or should be of 685 men ... each battalion is also decreased by 2 companies of grenadiers, one of 50 which forms the Grenadiers Royaux, and the other of 60 which make up what are called *grenadiers postiches* ['false grenadiers', employed to bring the regiments of the Grenadiers Royaux up to two battalions apiece]. The King has 222 squadrons, including his household cavalry and his gendarmerie, which total ... 21 squadrons.[2]

The orders received from Versailles urged the *Maréchal* to meet and defeat the army of the Duke of Cumberland, headquartered at Hanover. Cumberland had 48,000 Hanoverians, Hessians, and Brunswickers in the pay of Britain along with Prussians from the former Wesel garrison. This so-called Army of Observation has already assembled 25 battalions and 34 squadrons on a north-south axis between Nienburg and Hameln. To prevent the French from penetrating further into Westphalia, a party was preparing to set up at the Bielefeld camp, 40 kilometres further west towards Münster, where three Hanoverian regiments had already arrived.

Maréchal d'Estrées had hoped to force the enemy into repassing the Weser, but the state of supplies did not allow it. The time spent laying siege to Wesel was intended to build up these supplies but with Wesel evacuated, the army was flatfooted and not yet ready to move to the gates of Hanover. The *Maréchal* thought it was impossible to leave the banks of the Rhine before 25 May, unless Münster was threatened. In this case, if urgently needed, his intention was to send 26 more battalions to the Lippe while withdrawing what was already in Lippstadt down to Hamm. Upon his arrival, *Maréchal* d'Estrées took an interest in the situation at Geldern. His engineers had recognized that the flooding around the town was avoidable, he decided to conduct a siege on good ground and dedicate 17 battalions to it, starting on 1 May. Command of the siege was entrusted to the Marquis d'Armentières, *lieutenant-général*, who decided to establish several large camps.[3] Wesel was besieged the same day. Almost all the cavalry were behind. The cavalry regiments that left Maubeuge, Valenciennes and Sedan were directed to Roermond where they would form a camp of 34 *escadrons* under the orders of the Duc de Chaulnes, *lieutenant-général*, assisted by the Comtes de Guiche and Verceil as well as the Marquis de Barbançon and de Lastic, *maréchaux de camp*. The first of these cavalry regiments arrived at their destination on 6 May and the last did not reach the camp until the 22nd:

The troops set up camps ... in Düsseldorf, Neuss, Roermond, Wesel and we are thus divided to be able to survive more easily. However, subsistence is becoming increasingly scarce and the country we have behind, and in front of us even

---

2   Duc de Luynes, *Mémoires du duc de Luynes*, Vol.XV, p.399.
3   With him was the Duc d'Antin, the Comtes d'Orlick and de Sparre, Marquis de Dreux and de Leyde, Chevalier de Maupeou, *maréchaux de camp*. His corps comprised the Austrian regiment of Los Rios (1 battalion), and the Régiments d'Eu (2), Picardie (4), la Marine (4), Dauphin (2), Périgord (1), Grenadiers Royaux d'Aulan (1) and 300 men from ther artillery battalions of Menonville and La Motte.

more so, is perfectly capable of frightening an army smaller than ours. No doubt supplies will descend by the Meuse and the Rhine, and the means will be found to carry them to ahead of our army or with it when it marches.[4]

The French army was positioned from north to south thusly. The Prince of Beauvau with eight battalions in Münster and surrounding plain for communications on the Lippe. The Comte de Saint-Germain, the most advanced in the east, with eight battalions and four squadrons at Lippstadt and the north bank of the Lippe. There were eight other battalions and two squadrons between the Lippe and the Ruhr, at Lünen sur la Lippe, Dortmund further south and Unna 10 kilometres to the east, as well as Schwerte and Herdecke on the Ruhr. There were eight battalions and two squadrons behind them, on the east bank of the Rhine facing Düsseldorf, in the Duchy of Berg. Finally, to the west there were 50 battalions and 20 squadrons arranged from Wesel to Roermond between the Rhine and the Meuse, who were awaiting the arrival of fresh troops, bringing the total to 110 battalions and 127 squadrons.

The general officers in Wesel returned to their various corps. The army were not lacking senior officers. There 46 *lieutenant-généraux* and 65 *marechaux de camp*, compared to just 36 brigades and seven larger divisions (the two wings, the centre of the first and second lines, plus the reserve). The number of general officers was completely out of proportion with the numbers of troops so that most of them were not attached to a division or brigade, taking turns following a rotation table:

> They could not use them all; the *général-en-chef*, having a free choice, appointed officers with whom he had the most confidence to direct his detached corps, or those who enjoyed favour at court and so were recommended to him. Their comrades, jealous of this preference, with no other occupation than the ordinary routine of marches and camps, unnecessarily encumbered the staff. The presence of these idlers at headquarters, the tone of denigration they introduced there, their excessive pretensions, the grabbing of means of transport, the pomp of their existence, caused as much disruption as disorder and indiscipline, hindering the actions of the commander, undermining his authority, the mobility of the army and military spirit.[5]

On 4 May, the Prince de Soubise left to join the reserve corps entrusted to him, at Hamm on the Lippe, a little behind Lippstadt. He had separate staff but remained subordinate to *Maréchal* d'Estrées, who sent him a reinforcement of the Corps Royal de l'Artillerie with 10 guns. On the same day the enemy advanced with 4-5,000 men on Rietberg, 20 kilometres north of Lippstadt. *Maréchal* d'Estrées responded by advancing fresh troops south of the Lippe and occupied Lünen, Dortmund and Schwerte with six battalions. The Comte de Saint-Germain still occupied Lippstadt and the same posts along the north bank of the Lippe. *Generalmjaor* Graf von Schulenburg, of the

---

4   Chapotte, *Sous Louis le Bien-Aimé*, p.22.
5   Waddington, *La guerre de Sept ans*, p.393.

Hanoverian army, marched on Marienberg Abbey to take the grain and fodder stored there. Alerted by the presence of 300 Hanoverian cuirassiers on the Marienfeld side, a detachment of 50 Chasseurs de Fischer, half on foot, half on horseback, were sent to reconnoitre under the orders of a *capitaine* and a *lieutenant*. On the way they learned that the enemy was leaving Warendorf after causing a great deal of disorder there. When the mounted chasseurs reached the 120 Hanoverian cuirassiers, they drove them from Harsewinkel. The Hanoverians had formed in line at the end of the village. *Lieutenant* de Marsin, with his horsemen, and *Capitaine* de Cléry, with his infantrymen, attacked together with so much force that they put the cuirassiers to flight, causing them to fall back to their infantry supports. Thirty Hanoverians were killed, including an officer, and 10 prisoners taken including a wounded officer, the French chasseurs only had *Lieutenant* de Marsin wounded, and a few killed or wounded horses quickly replaced by those taken from the enemy. The same day, *Maréchal* d'Estrées recounted the skirmish in a letter to the minister stressing that 'this first action deserves some attention, because this troops behaved with great intelligence and valour' and that 'the prisoners have said that M. de Cumberland was at the camp and that had wished to march forward'.[6]

As the Duke of Cumberland arrived in Bielefeld with 10,000 men, the Comte de Saint-Germain brought the French left on the Lippstadt closer to Lippe. The *Maréchal* brought forward six battalions to Haltern and Dorsten and ordered that the movement to support the city of Münster by 20 battalions in case of threat, announced to the Minister as scheduled for 10 May, would be brought forward and carried out in two days' time.

On 5 May, the Marquis d'Armentières, who had come to Wesel to talk to *Maréchal* d'Estrées, returned to Guelders to make final arrangements for the blockade:

> The garrison made two sorties but achieved nothing. From time to time they fire a few cannon shots at the blockading troops, when they think they can distinguish Austrian uniforms. They do not shoot at the French. All soldiers who are working or on guard should wear French uniforms. All the monks and residents who did not have enough food for three months were sent outside the walls. This reveals they will hold out for a long time. They have done well to get rid of its useless mouths, but the blockading troops did wrong to let them pass. They should have forced them back by threats or musket. Their parents and friends would have forced the governor to take them back.[7]

The siege of Geldern was finally abandoned in favour of a simple blockade so as not to tie down too many troops. The Marquis d'Armentières left the Comte de Beausobre, *maréchal de camp*, in command with a Walloon battalion from the Austrian regiment of Los Rios, two battalions of Lowendahl and one of Périgord, tasked with building several redoubts.

---

6   Service historique de la défense (SHD), A1-3431.81. Post script, *Maréchal* d'Estrées to Minister of War, Wesel, 5 May 1757, 5:00 p.m.
7   Chapotte, *Sous Louis le Bien-Aimé*, p.26.

Passing through the Austrian Netherlands, [the army] first moved into Kleve to besiege the small town of Gueldre [Geldern], defended by 800 Prussians. It was expected that stopping the army, or part of it, to take this habitation would be a waste of time which would delay the general allied operations. As such, we took a party to build redoubts on the approaches to this small place and two battalions were left to guard them and prevent any food from entering and we sent fifty horses to aid these two battalions. This resolution was correct as one month later the garrison had consumed its provisions and, unable to hope for help, was forced to surrender the place and were taken as prisoners of war.[8]

On 6 May, the Prince de Soubise went to Lippstadt from Hamm to see the state of the place personally and the works that the Comte de Saint-Germain had undertaken there with the 10 battalions at his disposal. Both the garrison and those nearby could shelter in the works if needed. On 8 May several Hanoverian regiments arrived below the Weser while the six battalions destined for Dorsten and Haltern were still advancing along the north bank of the Lippe to support the posts around Hamm near the reserve of the Prince de Soubise. *Maréchal* d'Estrées crossed the Rhine to several other regiments which had hitherto remained between the Rhine and Meuse to make camps near Dorsten and Haltern and so reinforce Wesel. The Dorsten camp was already 11 battalions strong. Wesel, with 13 battalions and 12 squadrons, was to be augmented as troops arrived, sometimes after almost a month of marching and not in the best state to begin the campaign. As one officer wrote:

> We left Strasbourg on the 25th of this month and we are staying today [30 April] here in Landau. We have had thirty-two days of marching. Tomorrow we will enter the Palatinate and from there into the lands of the Queen of Hungary. We do not yet know where we will be camping. I will let you know this when we arrive. I will tell you that my servant has just deserted me at the very time when I needed him most and, my mount horse being very ill, I was obliged to take another one and give some very considerable pledges.[9]

The Duke of Cumberland advanced from Bielefeld, where he was entrenched with 22,000 men, on 10 and 11 May to Versmold and Rheda in the direction of Münster and Hamm, observing the slow and methodical advance of the French. Cumberland remained in control of the lower Bishopric of Münster, where he drew almost all of his subsistence. He multiplied his detachments which, gathering fodder and raising contributions, would take as much food as possible from Westphalia and the possessions of the Elector of Cologne.

The French army's main concern continued to be supporting the horses of the cavalry and the baggage train. *Maréchal* d'Estrées was very cautious about the ability of the mounted troops to survive in the country and did not look favourably on the Prince de Soubise's advance on Lippstadt, preferring to

---

8   Vogüé & Sourd, *Campagnes de Mercoyrol de Beaulieu*, p.110.
9   Randon Dulandre, an officer at Landau, to his brother at Saint-Jean de Bruel, 30 April 1757 (private collection).

wait a little longer before marching forward towards Münster. The quantities of fodder were not yet sufficient to be able to constitute supply stores that would make it possible to last the winter; 300,000 rations were expected in Münster but only 22,000 had been delivered. *Maréchal* de Belle-Isle had written from Paris urging an advance on the Weser. D'Estrées replied, 'If I advance in this season, I will destroy the King's army and I will eat without the resources of this country … you know the impossibility of using the army before the scythe can provide me with subsistence'.[10] He explained that instead he was going to 'take part of the forage from the houses and castles of some of the principal figures of the regency of Münster … When one has a march of 45 leagues to make, to supply food in advance of oneself, to carry heavy artillery anywhere and place it to serve usefully, it is impossible to steal.'[11] Nevertheless he advanced the infantry encamped in Dorsten under the orders of the Marquis de Villemur, *lieutenant-général*, to join the troops at the Haltern camp and to move on Dülmen, about 30 kilometres southwest of Münster, to deny the enemy the chance of taking any subsistence before they could arrive. He would do the same himself with the troops camped at Wesel if the enemy advanced further. At the same time, great parties of reconnaissance were dispatched to determine the exact position of the Duke of Cumberland's army, focussing south of Lippstadt as far as Warburg towards Cassel in the south-east and Arnsberg in the south-west:

> MM. de Vault and de Greaulme will leave Hamm on the 13th to go the same day to Erwitte. At Erwitte, each will be given twenty-five dragoons of the Volontaires Royaux; one of them will go via Gesecke to reach Büren the same day, the other will follow the main road from Erwitte to Büren. They will both take great care to note the nature of the country and its resources, the type of roads and the means that there would be to restore them, as well as the exact distances from all the places they pass through. Whoever passes through Gesecke may be able to learn news from the enemy, and if there is anything interesting, he would send it to Erwitte to pass on to the Prince de Soubise. They will meet in Büren, from where they will report with the detachment of the Volontaires Royaux right on Warburg by the main road from Paderborn to Cassel and will try to arrive there on the 15th; they will take, along the way, all the information discussed above on all points which may lead to the Weser and will stop at Warburg only as long as necessary to fulfil their purpose; as this is not far from Cassel, they will inquire, before arriving there, if the Hessians have any advanced troops, and as they are not going there to fight, they should not go as far as Warburg and Volkmarsen and try to get back to Brilon leaving these two places on their left. From Brilon they will send the Volontaires Royaux back to Erwitte, and also in Brilon they will find two companies of grenadiers from the Régiment de Reding who will escort them to Meschede, from which the two grenadier companies will continue to Erwitte. They will find in Meschede the grenadiers of [the Régiments de] Poitou

---

10   D'Estrées to Soubise, 6 May 1757 in Waddington, *La guerre de Sept ans*, p.395.
11   D'Estrées to Belle-Isle, 12 May 1757 in Waddington, *La guerre de Sept ans*, p.396.

and Saint-Germain who will escort them to Arnsberg, where they will find the two companies of grenadiers from which this detachment had been drawn.[12]

On 15 May, the regiment of Grenadiers de France, which was part of the Wesel garrison, were sent to the second line with the Grenadiers Royaux. Twenty-six battalions and 16 squadrons remained at the Wesel camp where the artillery park was also located. 'Infantry and dragoons come to us every day; but almost all the cavalry remained behind in Roermond and Düsseldorf, because of the lack of forage'.[13]

With the enemy seemingly unwilling to move, the *Maréchal* remained at the Wesel camp for some time while preparing to move forward. The Marquis de Villemur was still encamped at Dülmen; the Marquis de Laval, *maréchal de camp*, was in Haltern with six battalions and six squadrons. Until 20 May, the location of the 113 battalions and 143 squadrons of the auxiliary army, known as the Armée du Bas Rhin (Army of the Lower Rhine), was as follows:

Corps de Réserve. — 16 battalions comprising of the Régiments de Belzunce (4), Poitou (2), Provence (2), Salis-Suisse (2), Reding-Suisse (2), Alsace (3), Saint-Germain (1). — 24 squadrons comprising of the Régiments de Mestre-de-Camp-Général (2), Royal-Allemand (2), Saluces (2), Condé (2), Beauvilliers (2), Lameth (2), Wurtemberg (2), Nassau (2), le Roi (2), Marcieu (2), Cuirassiers du Roi (2) and la Rochefoucauld (2).

Corps de Münster. — Six battalions comprising of the Régiments de La Couronne (2), Vastan (2) and Conti (2).

Camp at Haltern. — Six battalions comprising of the Régiment d'infanterie de Chartres (2) also the Grenadiers Royaux de Modène and de Chantilly (4). — Four squadrons of the Régiments de Berri (2) and Bourbon (2).

Camp at Dorsten. — 11 battalions of the Régiments de Nassau-Sarrebruck (1), Royal-Bavière (2), Enghien (2), Orléans (2), Eu (2), Royal-Pologne (1) and the Menonville-Artillerie battalion (1). — Six squadrons of the Régiments de Clermont-Tonnerre (2), Bellefonds (2) and Royal-Pologne (2).

Camp at Wesel. — 35 battalions of the Régiments Roi (4), Picardie (4), Champagne (4), La Marine (4), Lyonnais, (2), Dauphin (2), Bergeret (2), Gardes Lorraine (2), Navarre (4), La Motte-Artillerie (1) Grenadiers de France (4) and Grenadiers Royaux d'Aulan (2) — 24 squadrons of the Régiments de Henrichemont (2), Commissaire-Général (2) Talleyrand (2) et Bourbon-Busset (2), also the Régiments de Dragons d'Orléans (4), Harcourt (4), Mestre-de- Camp-Général (4) and Colonel-Général (4).

---

12 Instruction from M. de Broglie to the *aides-maréchaux généraux des logis* de Vault and de Greaulme, 13 May 1757, in Pajol, *Les guerres sous Louis XV*, Vol.IV, p.62.
13 'Bulletin de l'armée du bas Rhin de Wesel le 14 mai', in Duc de Luynes, *Mémoires du duc de Luynes*, Vol.XVI, p.59.

HASTENBECK 1757

Fusilier, Régiment Royal-Bavière. Nineteenth-century watercolour by Charles Lyall. (Anne S.K. Brown Collection)

Detached infantry. — 39 battalions: Saxe-Gotha (1, Austrian), Prince de Ligne (1, Austrian) and Royal-Suédois (2) were stationed on the Lippe; La Dauphine (1) and Mailly (4) at Herdeke and Schwerte sur la Ruhr; Aquitaine (2), Bentheim (2) and Cambrésis (1) at Lünen and its surroundings; Condé (2), Arberg (1, Austrian), Courten-Suisse (2) at Wesel and on the Ruhr; Lochman-Suisse (2), Vaubécourt (2), la Roche-Aymon (2), Berg (1), Nassau- Usingen (1), la Mark (2) et Artillerie (1) at Cologne; Jenner-Suisse (2) at Ruremonde; Los Rios (1, Austrian), Foix (1), Périgord (1) and Lowendahl (4) were blockading Geldern.

Detached cavalry. — 24 squadrons: Royal (2), Maugiron (2), Dragons d'Aubigné (4) and le Roi-Dragons (4) on the Lippe; Hussards de Bercheny (4), Turpin (4) and Polleretsky (4) the heights of Cologne.

Camp at Düsseldorf. — 27 squadrons of the Régiments d'Aquitaine (2), Fumel (2), de Vienne (2), Carabiniers (10), Moustier (2), Royal-Roussillon (2), Colonel-Général (3), Bourgogne (2) and Dampierre (2).

Camp at Ruremonde, on the Meuse. — 34 squadrons of the Régiments de Clermont-Prince (2), Dauphin-Étranger (2), d'Archiac (2), Lenoncourt (2), Royal-Piémont (2), Royal-Étranger (2), Harcourt (2), Charost (2), Noailles (2), Royal-Cravates (2), Hainaut (2), Dauphin (2), Conti (2), la Reine (2), d'Escars (2), Fleury (2) and Orléans (2).

Despite this dispersion, provisions were still a problem and also seemed to determine the positions of the Duke of Cumberland. *Capitaine* Chapotte wrote:

> My regiment [Dauphin-Cavalerie] is encamped in Roermond ... There are six cavalry regiments here and more due to arrive; they only received half rations. This diet will put them in bad shape for the campaign. The King's stores are lacking, and private individuals are loaded with provisions which are good, and they sell to us cheaply. Entrepreneurs want to get rich quick ... All the troops that will make up this army have not yet arrived, and a great cause is that food is lacking [for them]. We must therefore wait until it arrives from the Meuse and the Rhine, before thinking about making any movements. We must also collect enough carts for transport, the Lippe is only able to carry small boats that can only pass to Lünen, and there is not half of what is needed; we have relied a little too much on the subsistence that the country would provide ... The Duke of Cumberland crossed and returned over the Weser, it seems that the object of this passage was only to consume the supplies of the country from the Weser to Lippstadt.[14]

On 18 May, the Prince de Soubise reported that the Duke of Cumberland was crossing the Weser with 10-12,000 men who appeared to be approaching Paderborn on the Lippe, 30 kilometres east of Lippstadt. The Comte de Saint-Germain was able to leave 10 battalions in the supply depot, but there was

---

14 Chapotte, *Sous Louis le Bien-Aimé*, pp.24-26.

every reason to believe that the enemy was looking primarily to consume or remove the grain and fodder from the Bishopric of Paderborn. Rather than heading for Lippstadt, *Maréchal* d'Estrées was still constrained by supplies which prevented him from mustering his infantry. He preferred to take his army corps to Münster then return to take an intermediate position in the direction of Hamm, and asked the Prince de Soubise to leave his billets, assemble his cavalry, gather intelligence on enemy movements and put himself in a position to support Lippstadt. *Maréchal* d'Estrées would set out on 21 May and estimated to be able to be between Münster and Hamm on the 25th with 48 battalions and 20 squadrons plus 20 battalions and eight squadrons in a second line, ready to join him. The *Maréchal* then hoped to join the Prince de Soubise's corps at Warendorf and threaten the Duke of Cumberland sufficiently to persuade him to return over the Weser:

> M. de Soubise advanced into the country of Munster at the head of his 24,000 men, followed at two intervals by 40 battalions. He marched along the Lippe towards Lippstadt. If he continued, he would meet the Duke of Cumberland who crossed the Weser at the head of 30-50,000 men and would contest the difficult ground and the defiles that they have occupied. It seems that the whole army will have to come together if we want to force the difficult approaches.[15]

On 20 May, the Hanoverian troops of the Army of Observation were at Lippspringe and advanced about 10 kilometres below Paderborn, a large, fairly fortified town, where they stopped for the next few days. As a result, the Prince de Soubise, who had left Hamm and encamped under Lippstadt, believed he could wait for *Maréchal* d'Estrées. He took the precaution of advancing the six battalions which were in Dortmund under the orders of the Chevalier de Muy, *lieutenant-général,* and five others who were in Haltern with the Duc de Laval, *maréchal de camp,* to Hamm. Further back, the Marquis de Souvré, *lieutenant-général,*[16] advanced on Münster from Wesel with 18 battalions of the Gardes Lorraine (2), Picardie (4), La Marine (4), Dauphin (2), Lyonnais (2) and Champagne (4). Camps were established on the 21st at Schermbeck on the Lippe, 20 kilometres east of Wesel, on the 22nd at Lembeck 14 kilometres north of Dorsten, then Dülmen, 13 kilometres north-east of Haltern on 23 May where the troops stayed put as it was raining heavily. The Comte de Gisors wrote:

> Yesterday, leaving Lembeck, we marched in two columns … Arrived at two o'clock in the morning on the edge of a small river which is half a league below our camp. M. de la Vauguyon, who was leading us, ordered us to stop and let all the *équipages* pass in front of us.[17] Note that it was raining heavily, our soldiers were

---

15 Chapotte, *Sous Louis le Bien-Aimé*, p.22.
16 François Louis Le Tellier de Louvois, Marquis de Souvré (1704-1767) was youngest son of Louis XIV's secretary of state for war and was made *maréchal de camp* in 1743 and a *lieutenant-général* in 1748.
17 Translators note: *Équipages* is the collective noun which refers to the waggoners and suppliers who kept the army logistics moving as well as officers' servants moving their own personal

cold, and they had no bread or meat left. For two hours I waited patiently. Only the *équipages* of eight battalions had passed during this time because there were many large crews mixed up into small detachments and at any moment a cart got stuck or a horse fell. We took it upon ourselves, the Marquis de Villeroy [*colonel* of the Régiment de Lyonnais] and I [*colonel* of the Régiment de Champagne], to go and find M. de la Vauguyon. He was in a village on the edge of river where he was warming himself, and we represented to him that our soldiers, being weary of the cold and the misery, ran the risk of remaining there until six in the evening if he wanted us to wait until all the *équipages* had gone past. M. de la Vauguyon was convinced by our reasons and gave orders to the Régiment de Lyonnais, which was to lead the resumed march. Champagne followed. My first battalion was beginning to enter the village, when I was ordered to go back to the place where I had stopped; I immediately retreated and started again. After 5 or 6 minutes, I was ordered to march forward again. I champed at the bit and we set off again, about face; finally, two battalions of the regiment having already passed the village, we stopped the other two in the village itself, scattered in small platoons, and in this position we remained in the rain until five o'clock, until the last donkey of the army passed by.[18]

The army continued its advance on the 25th on Apelhülsen, 18 kilometres west of Münster. This march had been preceded by a letter requesting the passage of the army to 'the general officer of the Hanoverian troops' who replied on behalf of the Duke of Cumberland, from Bielefeld, on 15 May that the aim of his army was as much to preserve the interests of the Elector as to prevent the passage of any troops into his estates. The question of Hanover's neutrality was finally settled.

The Duke of Cumberland remained in place for several days. Of his 44 battalions and as many squadrons he had scarcely half with him; at Bielefeld there was a Prussian brigade, and some at Rietberg to cover the communications with the corps encamped at Paderborn. The rest were enroute, or in Hanover.

On the 23 May the Comte de Maillebois arrived at Münster. On the 24th he set out to reconnoitre the course of Upper Ems from Telgte, 5 kilometres east of Münster, to Rheda-Wiedenbrück. He returned after having 'reconnoitred the enemy position and opened the route which the *Maréchal* will need for the movements he is preparing' to force the enemy to abandon his position and prevent him from consuming the last fodder.[19] Having marched through Dorsten and Haltern to scout this part of the Lippe, *Maréchal* d'Estrées arrived at Münster on the 26th where he established his headquarters and a camp in several lines, between the city of Münster and the river Wene, to the east. Relations between the authorities and the *commissaire des guerres* remained complicated due to a lack of premises which they did not want to

---

baggage. Logistic services were undertaken by private contractors and would not become a formalised part of the army until the Napoleonic era.
18   Gisors to Belle-Isle, Dülmen, 24 May 1757 in Waddington, *La guerre de Sept ans*, p.401.
19   SHD, archives du génie, Série 1 V, Article 15, section 1, dossier 5, pièce 23: Journal de la campagne de 1757.

provide, forcing a hospital to be set up in the Jesuit college. The 18 battalions brought from Wesel by the Marquis de Souvré joined those of the Marquis de Villemur in Dülmen. The Duc d'Orleans had departed on 25 May and arrived on the 30th with the rest of the troops from the Wesel camp.

As for the cavalry, 16 squadrons finally arrived in Münster on 28 May and established themselves in the northeast of the town. The Duc de Brissac, *lieutenant-général*, advanced from his camp at Neuss towards Wesel on the 29th and 30th. The camp at Roermond under the orders of the Duc de Ayen, *lieutenant-général*, was held a few days, despite the idleness which reigned there, as described by Chapotte:

> [F]or more than a month since the regiment has been encamped in this place, I have only been on duty once, in kind of service called *piquet*, which was not arduous, on horseback from time to time out of convenience for my horses and to keep me from boredom. This boredom is a terrible business for those who do not know what to do, I see the fatigue it causes many of the men around me.[20]

On 30 May the Prince de Soubise gave an account of his position at Lippstadt and the enemy to the Minister of War:

> I have not written to you for a few days, as our position has remained the same as a consequence of the enemies inaction; they are still in their camp before Paderborn; the day before yesterday I went to reconnoitre it, with a detachment of Volontaires Royaux, on a height in front of Salzkotten from where we could see the right and the left of their camp perfectly, and everyone agreed an estimate that there were at least 15-18,000 men; some dragoons of my escort approached their mounted sentries and larger guards and not one fired a shot; as my object was to calmly scout the country, I forbade an attack: thus I had time to examine their position, which seems very good; I do believe, however, that one could easily turn left passing the Alme river some distance above, but it would be an operation which would require greater forces than I have. The right of their camp goes as far as Neuhaüs and the left covers Paderborn.[21]

At the end of May, the Armée du Bas Rhin was assembled in front of Münster while the 26 battalions and 18 squadrons of the reserve were still at Lippstadt, where they could follow by a short march. Light troops lined the Ems, which flowed from Rietberg to Emsdetten, through Rheda-Wiedenbrück, Warendorf, Telgte and Greven; some detachments pushed beyond the Ems to reconnoitre and observe the movements of the enemy, whose main body remained entrenched in Brackwede, two kilometres in front of Bielefeld. A second corps remained in readiness at Paderborn, to the south-east.

From Münster, *Maréchal* d'Estrées took care of the arrangements for his plans, which he thought could only be achieved in the first days of June without becoming delayed since the plans established before the opening of the campaign specified that he could not go further than Münster before 1

---

20   Chapotte, *Sous Louis le Bien-Aimé*, pp. 43-44.
21   Pajol, *Les guerres sous Louis XV*, Vol.IV, pp.63-64.

June. This supposed that there were stores in the city when there was not actually a third of what was hoped for. The difficulty of subsisting would be extreme when moving away from the Rhine. *Maréchal* de Turenne had had to face the same difficulties in his time, but he had only 25,000 men subsisting in Westphalia; now there were well over 100,000 men without counting the useless mouths that inevitably follow the army. The *Maréchal* believed that on 6 June, after three days march, he would be able to force the enemy to retreat or fight.

Yet from the first weeks of the campaign, disagreement had arisen between d'Estrées and his *maréchal général de logis*. The Comte de Maillebois took advantage of his admissions to court and his father-in-law, the Marquis de Paulmy, Secretary of State for War, and never ceased to denounce what he called 'the irresolution, the contradictions which reign here' as well as the incompetence of his leader who he wanted replaced by his friend, the Duc de Richelieu.[22] This cabal benefited from the support of Madame de Pompadour because the Prince de Soubise, her protégé, had been very disappointed not to receive independent command. These denunciations came at an auspicious time. During the month and a half since the *Maréchal*'s arrival with the army, the lack of movement had been impressed on the feelings of Versailles.

---

22 Maillebois to de Paulmy, 26 May 1757 in Waddington, *La guerre de Sept ans*, p.403. Louis-François-Armand du Plessis (1696-1788), Duc de Richelieu and later Duc de Fronsac, grand-nephew of the Cardinal. A *maréchal de France* since 1748, he 'shouted loudly' in the words of Cardinal Bernis when the King chose the Comte d'Estrées to command the army.

5

The Main Operation

A general who leads a French army into Germany must think of a means to provide subsistence to assure a retreat in case of misfortune.[1]

In the first days of June, *Maréchal* d'Estrées had 67 battalions and 37 squadrons around Münster, while the Prince de Soubise occupied Lippstadt with 20 battalions and 20 squadrons.

Composition of the Münster camp. — 54 battalions of the Régiments de Navarre (4), La Marine (4), Champagne (4), Le Roi (4), Lyonnais (2), Gardes Lorraine (2), Dauphin (2), Picardie (4), Enghien (2), Vastan (2), La Couronne (2), Chartres (2), Royal-Pologne (1), Condé (2), Conti (2), Eu (2), Royal-Baviére (2) and Orléans (2) as well as the Grenadiers de France (4), Grenadiers Royaux (4) and the Corps Royal de l'Artillerie (1). — 28 squadrons of the Régiments Royal (2), Berry (2), Bellefonds (2), Henrichemont (2), Royal-Pologne (2), Talleyrand (2), Bourbon-Busset (2), Clermont-Tonnerre (2), Commissaire-Général (2) and Bourbon (2) as well as the Régiments de Dragons Colonel-Général (4) and Orléans (4).

Thus entrenched, the *Maréchal* 'must not fear being attacked there by the Duke of Cumberland because Lippstadt, located in the marshes, could not accommodate many, making it unassailable as Münster is too far from the Weser for the enemy to dare go there in force'.[2]

For his part, the Duke of Cumberland was at the head of some 22,000 men at Bielefeld and Rietberg. On his left there was a corps of 10-12,000 men encamped at Paderborn, further south. This holding position was not without tactical advantages, as enumerated by Chapotte:

> It seems to me that the views of M. de Cumberland … are: 1° to hold the *Maréchal* to advance troops and leave the vicinity of the Rhine earlier than he wanted and perhaps lacking subsistence; 2° To encourage his army by this bold step and

---

[1] De Retzow, *Nouveaux memoires*, p.220. Retzow added that 'a general is to be pitied, when his merit does not serve as an aegis against the poison of the base schemers who besiege the throne of an indolent and characterless monarch!'

[2] Chapotte, *Sous Louis le Bien-Aimé*, p.27.

to intimidate those of his enemies; 3° To be in force and assembled, while the troops of M. d'Estrées are dispersed in different posts to fall on a few, if he finds the right opportunity; 4° To destroy all the subsistence in front of the Weser so that its enemies subsist with more difficulty and cannot hold there long; 5° To be within reach to harass the light troops and large detachments, food convoys, and magazines.[3]

However, the enemy seemed to be losing their tranquillity, occupying themselves with gathering and destroying fodder. They took 'the subsistence that time did not allow them to consume and [committing] disorders that were forbidden by the laws of war. not even in an enemy country'.[4] On the French side, it was believed that when the Duke of Cumberland saw the army assembled and able to survive, he 'would hurry to cross the Weser, but if he saw many troops assembled and no food to their rear, he would hold out where he was, harass them avoiding a large engagement' because the balance of forces was still unfavourable.[5]

From 3-5 June, the Armée du Bas Rhin began its advance on the Ems in incessant rain which made the roads difficult. Indiscipline became more and more common, The *Maréchal*, who did not want 'to be at the head of an army of thieves', was forced to severe judgement to deter marauding. He condemned perpetrators to death. The first line left Münster on 3 June to camp at Telgte then at Warendorf the next day, in the centre of the army's position, where the second line arrived on the 5th. The state given for the infantry of the Warendorf camp was a strength of 1,900 junior officers and 31,800 soldiers under arms, plus 1,400 soldiers in hospital. One officer wrote that:

> Our camp is very beautiful; the first line has its right supported against the town on a height which dominates the river Ems. The second line is on the other side of the main road, which makes a very good route for the columns. We had terrible rain, the whole country was flooded.[6]

A day later, and another account recording much the same:

> We are in a beautiful camp, but we cannot get out because of the difficulty of the roads, which are nothing more than abysses caused by the continual and abundant rains which have fallen for several days … The soldier suffers tremendously in the tent where he is in the mud up to his knee; he also suffers, or rather the officer, from the shortage of bread. You can't get it for money and it's going for 8 sols a livre. There is meat. We are starting to find some vegetables in the ground, and we have allowed some small forages to make up for the lack of hay and oats, which

---

3   Chapotte, *Sous Louis le Bien-Aimé*, p.27.
4   François Antoine Chevrier, *Histoire de la campagne de 1757 sur le Bas-Rhin dans l'Electorat d'Hanovre et autres pays conquis* (Francfort: Unknown Publisher, 1757), p.65.
5   Chapotte, *Sous Louis le Bien-Aimé*, p.29.
6   Letter from an unidentified officer, Warendorf, 6 June, in Duc de Luynes, *Mémoires du duc de Luynes*, Vol.XVI, pp.81-82.

HASTENBECK 1757

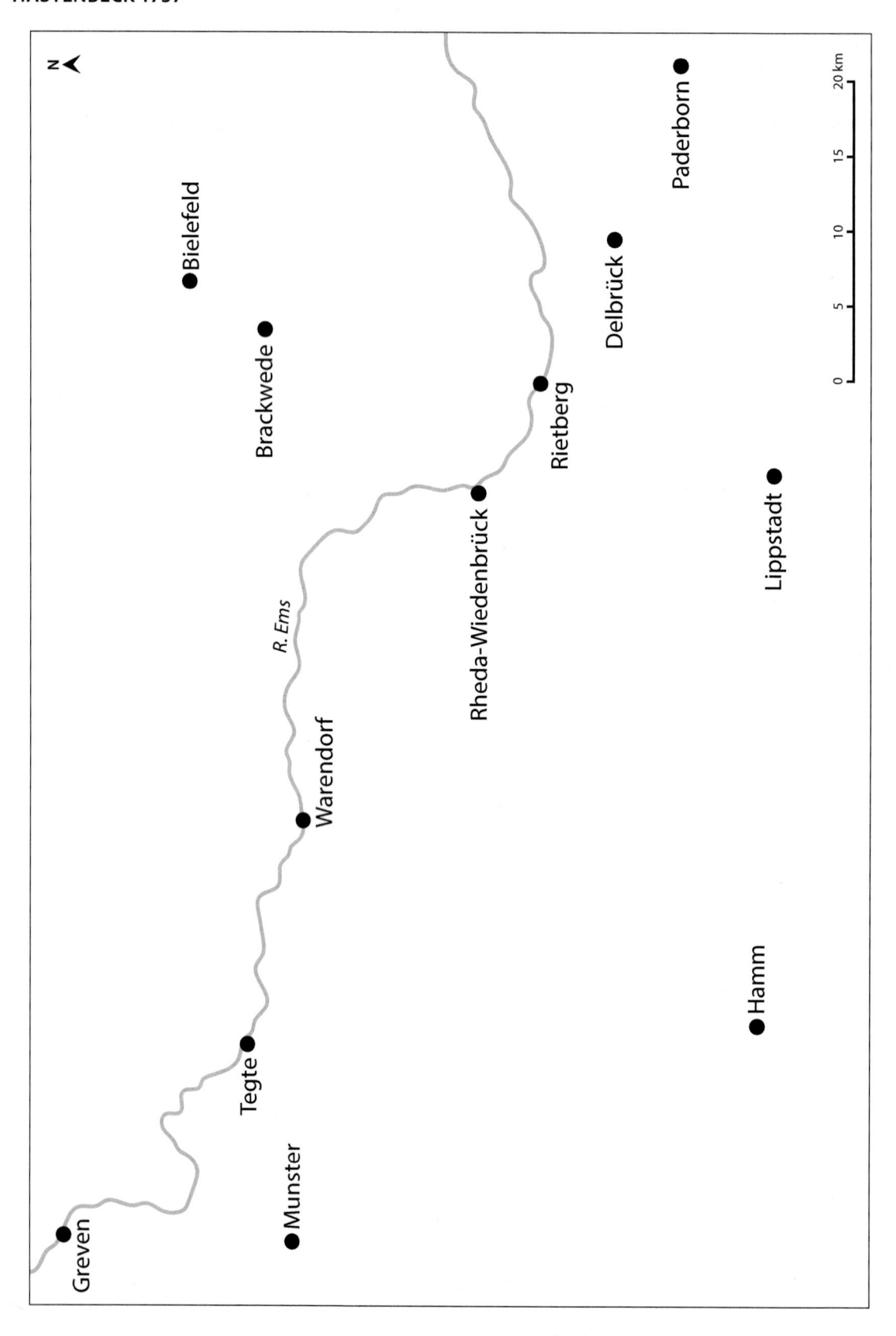

cannot arrive because of bad roads. All of Westphalia is swampy ground where it is not possible to wage war unless the season is more favourable.[7]

Eight battalions of Grenadiers Royaux and Grenadiers de France from the reserve remained at Telgte, on the left, with a regiment of dragoons. The Chevalier de Muy left Hamm on 2 June with 15 battalions to move to the right at Herzebrock, north-west of Rheda. Three battalions which could only leave their position by boat remained temporarily at the Owerhagen camp, near Lippstadt. A report of 4 June gave the strength of the army encamped in Westphalia as 86 battalions and 84 squadrons without counting the 19 battalions and 28 squadrons on the Rhine, or at the Roermond camp.

On 5 June, the Comte de Maillebois went to reconnoitre the enemy positions and moved with a detachment to Marienfeld Abbey:

> [F]rom the steeple of which the enemy camp could be seen in the open. It is halfway up the hill facing Marienfeld, guarding the entrance to Ravensberg and Herford Gorge on the right. It is said that there are large marshes on the right, and that the left is fortified by brick and stone embrasures. M. le *Maréchal* will either march into the front of them, or turn them.[8]

The same day, a *lieutenant* and 20 men of the Régiment de Bentheim went to gather fodder in the county of Tecklenbourg which had previously belonged to the Comte de Bentheim, their *colonel*. They were surprised and all but six of them were captured by a Hanoverian detachment.

Major operations began on 6 June when, feeling threatened, the Duke of Cumberland recalled *Generalleutnant* von Schmettau's corps of around 15,000 Hanoverians and Hessians from Paderborn to reunite with the 18,000 men encamped at Brackwede and Bielefeld, where the two Prussian regiments were encamped. The Prince de Soubise immediately realised that 'the enemy had decamped that night from Paderborn'. As he reported:

> I am going, while awaiting the orders of M. le *Maréchal*, to advance the [cavalry] brigade of Mestre-de-Camp-Général to Gesecke and to push the Volontaires Royaux as far as Paderborn to try to conserve what may remain of the fodder in the country and gain more certain news of the enemy. M. de Chabo is at Neuhaus and has driven detachments back to a coffee-house called Hollanderhaus on the way to Bielefeld; a column of the enemy was encamped half a league from this house and was now continuing on to Bielefeld via Wiedenbrück. M. de Bussy with his detachment of volunteers spent the night at Delbrück, I ordered him to approach as close as possible to Rietberg to find out whether the enemy has sent new reinforcements there and where they are camping in the vicinity of this town. M. Fischer is within reach of gathering information at Rheda and Wiedenbrück. The plan of M. d'Estrées being to force the enemies to retake the Weser, the retreat

---

7   Letter from an unidentified officer, Warendorf, 7 June, in Duc de Luynes, *Mémoires du duc de Luynes*, Vol.XVI, pp.81-82.
8   Letter from Warendorf, 6 June, Duc de Luynes, *Mémoires du duc de Luynes*, Vol.XVI, pp.81-82.

HASTENBECK 1757

Grenadiers Royaux. Formed from the grenadier companies of the Militia, their uniforms were distinguished from those of their parent units by the addition of epaulettes and a blue collar. (NYPL Vinkhuijzen Collection)

THE MAIN OPERATION

Trooper of the cavalry regiment Mestre-de-Camp-Général. (NYPL Vinkhuijzen Collection)

of the Hanoverians does not change the orderly movement to gather his army on the Ems.⁹

The rain stopped and the *Maréchal* concentrated his army to cross the Ems. The Prince de Soubise went to Wiedenbrück on 7 and 8 June with the 26 battalions and 20 squadrons of the reserve. Their encampments were now less than a league to the right of the rest of the army. The following night, the enemy evacuated 1,500 men from Rietberg. Fischer's corps, which occupied the abbey of Marienfeld, was attacked by 500 Hanoverian grenadiers and 200 cuirassiers. A company of chasseurs and a company of grenadiers forced the enemy to withdraw in haste with their fire; the Hanoverians lost several wounded and the commander of their four infantry companies was killed. Fischer's troop lost the *capitaine* of the company of chasseurs and two grenadiers killed, plus a *lieutenant* and two soldiers wounded. The *Maréchal*, at Rheda, learned of the enemy's evacuation of Rietberg the next day and immediately sent the Volontaires Royaux to invest the position; a company of Volontaires and Fischer's corps were placed in front, three kilometres from the enemy outposts. On 10 June, 55 battalions and 40 squadrons were on the Ems at Herzebrock, north of Rheda. The river crossing took place on the 12th at Rheda and Wiedenbrück, postponed by a day due to bad weather. The reserve advanced to Neuenkirchen, two kilometres north of Rietberg. The works which the Duke of Cumberland had erected, believed to be considerable, suggested his intention to hold the position:

> [I]t is said that the approach to the village of [Brackwede] is very well entrenched, that almost the entire front and the left of his camp were covered with impassable marshes, and that the right was fortified with several redoubts: the bold face of this general who, for several days had dared to stand firm in the face of our army, greatly helped to ensure the great ideas that we had of his camp.¹⁰

On the 13th, the *Maréchal* went to Neunkirchen to discuss the reconnaissance with the Prince de Soubise. He decided to march on the enemy's left flank as soon as possible, which was on 18 June. The Comte de Lillebonne advanced on the enemy's right with Fischer's corps and 700 dragoons; 300 Volontaires Royaux advanced between Rheda and Bielefeld and eight companies went to Marienfeld; the rest of the Volontaires went to Gütersloh and the hussars from Turpin further on to Holte Castle.¹¹

The movement around Bielefeld did not escape the view of the Duke of Cumberland. Knowing his position was rather weak and fearing an attack on his left which would cut him off from the Weser, he felt he should not wait and decided to retreat east towards the river. On 13 June, around 6:00 p.m.,

---

9   Pajol, *Les guerres sous Louis XV*, Vol.IV, p.65.
10 Chapotte, *Sous Louis le Bien-Aimé*, p.52.
11 François Henri de Harcourt Beuvron, Comte de Lillebonne (1726-1802) had been *brigadier* since 1748 and *mestre de camp* of the Dragons d'Harcourt. He would become duc on November 2, 1757, a *maréchal de camp* in 1758 and *lieutenant-général* in 1762. He emigrated in 1790 and died in Great Britain.

he set out with his 46 battalions and 38 squadrons, withdrawing to Herford, 15 kilometres further north:

> His plan and his marches were so well disguised that he would have completely concealed this movement from the enemy, always dangerous when one is so close, without a servant of *Maréchal* d'Estrées who, not knowing what to do, took it into his head to go up the steps of a bell tower with a telescope to view this camp which was so talked about. This man spied more as a general rather than a servant, he saw that the troops of this camp were moving and disappearing; he ran to tell his master, who immediately sent several large detachments to charge the rear guard. As the pursuit began too late it could not have much success; M. Turpin entered the enemy camp with the hussars who looted some baggage; Bielefeld was looted, we found 8-10,000 rations, and ended with an equal loss of about 100 men killed on each side and about 3-400 prisoners that we took, the fruit that we took from one of the great opportunities to fight well that presented itself in war. Candour and good faith are undoubtedly the character of the *Maréchal*, he said on the spot and publicly the service that his servant had rendered him and our army, this event praised his heart more than his skill.[12]

Convinced that the enemy occupied a formidable position that it would hold, the French did not perceive the retreat early enough to be able to take advantage of it. Only the Volontaires Royaux of the Comte de Chabo, who were in Gütersloh and Marienfeld, managed to reach the Duke of Cumberland's rear-guard in the morning, after marching all night.

At dawn on 14 June, the Comte de Chabo took the last enemy detachments still in Bielefeld and forced them to withdraw abandoning several wagons, 8-10,000 thousand rations of fodder and several prisoners, including one officer and 100 men killed. A panicked Hanoverian cavalry regiment galloped off, overturning everything in its path. The enemy was pursued as far as Herford where they rallied to several rear-guard battalions that the Duke of Cumberland took care to leave in the town, surrounded by ramparts and ditches, to cover the retreat of the rest of his army beyond the Weser.

In the event the Volontaires Royaux lost 20 killed and wounded, including five officers having become over extended. Despite all their diligence, the reinforcement of 10 companies of grenadiers, 10 *piquets* and 300 horses, under the orders of the Prince de Beauvau, as well as 12 companies of grenadiers and 200 horses of the reserve, commanded by the Comte de Lorges, arrived exhausted, once the action was over. The French losses amounted to about 30 men and six officers for the price of 100 of the enemy along with 300 hundred deserters. In addition to the few army servants taken from the Bielefeld camp, large quantities of brandy, flour and fodder were also seized.

Maréchal d'Estrées immediately reported the events to the King:

> Sire, I have sought ways to force him [the Duke of Cumberland] to leave and cross the Weser; this could only be done by attacking him head-on in a camp prepared

---

12 Chapotte, *Sous Louis le Bien-Aimé*, pp.52-53.

long in advance, or by turning him to his left, the right being unassailable. The steps I took to fulfil this object were successful and I suspected to be four days from fighting an action which I was determined to give as soon as I recognized an opportunity. This resolution was stopped yesterday; M. de Cumberland did not see fit to wait any longer; he left yesterday at 4 o'clock in the evening; his army took the road to Herford, where I had several detachments followed him. I will move forward on Gütersloh to speed up his march across the Weser, while I establish at Paderborn for subsequent operations which has pleased Your Majesty to order me to do.[13]

Apart from the 4,000 men of the Comtes de Chabo, de Lorges and the Prince of Beauvau's three detachments, *Maréchal* d'Estrées had not taken any measures to harass the retreat of the Duke of Cumberland. No real pursuit went beyond Bielefeld against his rear-guard. The Prince de Beauvau's detachment did not leave until 11:00 p.m. the day before due to a misunderstanding and marched all night. Stopping at Bielefeld, known for its canvas factories, the soldiers engaged in looting 'which the officers could no longer repress' which prevented the detachment moving until the afternoon with the Volontaires Royaux of the Comte de Chabo.[14] In the meantime the Count de Lorges arrived and, finding bold defenders, did not go beyond Bielefeld. Only the Prince de Beauvau continued to advance with his detachment, as reported by the Comte de Gisors:

> The bridges of the river which could have been destroyed by the enemy rear-guard but were not, the quantity of deserters coming to us and the reports they made, the Berlin mail arriving from Hervorden [Herford] which we stopped and from which the enemy had not thought of withdrawing their letters, gave us reason to believe that they were in great confusion. We started off again at midnight in the firm hope of catching more from their rear-guard. The next day we received bad news from a new deserter who told us on the way that there were only 150 men left in Hervorden. However, instead of 150 men we saw nothing at all, and fifteen volunteers were killed after some ineffectual fire at the walls [of Hervorden]. We summoned the place [to surrender] without success, and after seeing enemy troops all day filing along the opposite bank of the river that we could not cross, we were forced to withdraw on the evening of the 15th, according to all the rules of prudence.[15]

The Comte de Lorges, who had erred on the side of caution the day before, did not follow the Prince de Beauvau in his retreat and, having remained at Herford until the next day, 16 June, which the enemy evacuated during the night. The entire Army of Observation made its way to its bridges over the Weser at Rheme and Vlotho, some 15 kilometres further northeast. The Duke of Cumberland crossed the river after removing all the grain and fodder as far as the Weser. He left only a few weak detachments below the

---

13   Letter from Rheda in Pajol, *Les guerres sous Louis XV*, Vol.IV, p.65.
14   Gisors to Belle-Isle, 29 June 1757 in Waddington, *La guerre de Sept ans*, p.408.
15   Gisors to Belle-Isle, 29 June 1757 in Waddington, *La guerre de Sept ans*, p.408.

river with the firm intention of keeping behind this natural barrier, which the Hanoverians considered difficult to cross but which now left the country of Hesse at the mercy of the French, and headed towards Minden. The Crown Prince of Hesse-Cassel who commanded the Prussian brigade under the orders of the Duke of Cumberland described, in his report to the King of Prussia, a very poor retreat:

> The Hanoverians, the Hessians and the Brunswick troops marched so fast to reach Herford that if the French army had come to support the attacking corps, our whole rear-guard would have been mauled. This is what these allied armies are like. In general, it seems that the Hanoverians are not good Prussians; I dare not entrust everything to the pen.[16]

On the French side, the Comte de Maillebois took the opportunity to continue his denigration of *Maréchal* d'Estrées who, however, 'treated him well [and] shown friendship and trust for six weeks'.[17] It was also at this time that the Prince de Soubise, who had disagreed with the *Maréchal* d'Estrées, was recalled to Paris accompanied by the Comte de Saint-Germain who was also under his orders in the reserve corps.

The King of Prussia had won a victory before Prague on 6 May and was now besieging the city. The allies had to avoid any more Prussian successes which would bring ruin to Austria. The raising of a second army of 60,000 men was decided. Part of this army would remain on the Upper Rhine reassuring the states of the Holy Roman Empire, and the other would act in Bohemia.

During the negotiations led by the Comte d'Estrées in Vienna, France had insisted on substituting an army of 100,000 men on the lower Rhine for an auxiliary corps of 24,000 men that would join with the Empress's armies. Austrian ministers stressed that such a diversion from Westphalia and Hanover would have no bearing on the war in Saxony and Bohemia. In strict application of the Treaty of Versailles and to keep his word, Louis XV would therefore send a second French army to Germany made up of troops from France and cavalry regiments from the Armée du Bas Rhin left in subsistence on the Rhine. More than 30,000 men were on their way from all over the kingdom to Alsace. Thirty battalions and 40 squadrons would be assigned to the army corps under the orders of the *Maréchal* Duc de Richelieu on the Upper Rhine, while 20 battalions and 18 squadrons arriving from Alsace would form a separate command entrusted to the Prince de Soubise. The latter would march on 20 July from Landau and Lauterbourg and, joined by 8,000 Austrians from Brabant, would cross the Rhine towards Koblenz to go to Erfurt where he would meet the troops of the Prinz von Sachsen-Hildburghausen and where the nearby Comte de Saint-Germain would be sent to plan the movement. 'This army is directed to the Elbe and, by various

---

16 'Rapport du prince de Hesse-Cassel au roi de Prusse', in Waddington, *La guerre de Sept ans*, p.411.
17 Comte de Maillebois to Marquis de Paulmy, secret correspondence, 14 June 1757 in Waddington, *La guerre de Sept ans*, p.410.

marches and without encountering enemies, it [will go] near Rosbach where the King of Prussia, with 25,000 men, has gone for the purpose of combat'.[18] Although twice the size of the Prussian army, this army was severely beaten at Rosbach on 5 November 1757.

Despite the constitution of a new army, *Maréchal* d'Estrées was only informed of Prince de Soubise's destination when he had received the order to go to Versailles. To the great satisfaction of its commander-in-chief who had also proposed to the minister to take as many as he wanted, several general officers left the Armée du Bas Rhin, where there was a plethora, for the upper Rhine. The Duc de Luynes recorded that:

> Thirteen *lieutenant-généraux* were fired from the army of *Maréchal* d'Estrées to be sent to that of M. de Richelieu and we were also joined by a [new] one, M. de la Chétardie; eighteen *maréchaux de camp* were also fired from this same army and three were added to it, MM. de Monti, de Roquépine and de Tresnel.[19]

The *Maréchal* took the opportunity to reorganize his reserve corps. He divided it into two new corps which he entrusted to two *lieutenant-generaux* and placed them according to the provisions of his courier from the king. The first, on the right, with three infantry brigades and as many cavalry, was under the orders of the Marquis d'Armentières, who was at Oerlinghausen and Detmold to cover Paderborn, 30 kilometres to the south where the Marquis de Dreux was with four battalions.[20] The second corps was on the left at Enger in the county of Ravensberg, 10 kilometres north-west of Herford, and was made up of two infantry brigades, as many cavalry and a regiment of dragoons, commanded by the Duc de Broglie.[21] It was intended to harass the enemy on the lower Weser opposite Minden while covering East Frisia where *Maréchal* d'Estrées had sent Broglie's detachment. The latter was thus able to target Minden and Hameln, attempt crossing the Weser to enter the Electorate of Hanover, or to cover the invasion of Hesse. The last mounted troops that had remained in subsistence behind at the Roermond camp, advanced on Wesel. Chapotte wrote:

> We have just received orders from the Court to leave tomorrow for a three day march to Wesel and to wait there until other orders are received: twelve squadrons of 32 will leave; the others seem to be destined for the Upper Rhine army: the latter are very happy with their fate; it is not the same with the former, we do not

---

18 Vogüé & Sourd, *Campagnes de Mercoyrol de Beaulieu*, p.110. The village of Rosbach or Roßbach was in the municipality of Braunsbreda in Saxony, 40 kilometres west of Leipzig.
19 Duc de Luynes, *Memoires du duc de Luynes*, Vol.XVI, p.95.
20 Armentiéres' infantry brigades were made up of the Régiments de Belzunce (4), Salis (2), Reding (2), Alsace (3) and Saint-Germain (1).
21 Louis Victor-François, second Duc de Broglie (1718-1804) was the eldest son of *Maréchal* François-Marie Duc de Broglie (1671-1745). Made a *maréchal de camp* in 1745, he had been *lieutenant-general* since 1748 and became *maréchal de France* and Prince of the Holy Empire on 13 April 1759, after the Battle of Bergen. Disgraced in 1761, he would become Louis XVI's Minister of War in 1789 and died in exile after the Revolution. His infantry brigades consisted of the Régiments de Poitou (2), Provence (2), Royal-Suédois (2) and Royal-Baviére (2).

go willingly to the army of M. d'Estrées where we expect to fall into fatigue and misery.[22]

The Armée du Bas Rhin left Rheda to settle in Gütersloh on 18 June, then Bielefeld on 20th. Boats and heavy artillery were summoned from Wesel to Lippstadt. However, at Versailles the mood was to display France as ready to deliver more than it had promised and there was also an effort to prove that action in Westphalia and Hanover was effective. As a result the most pressing orders were addressed to *Maréchal* d'Estrées to engage in battle against the Duke of Cumberland:

> Whatever reasons you may have for delaying the operations of your army to ensure an advantage, I am obliged to tell you that the King thinks that they must yield to the political views which in the present circumstances require that you strongly press the Duke of Cumberland, and that you promptly do something of brilliance … His Majesty therefore commands me very expressly to explain to you that he strongly desires you attempt to cross the Weser, and that if against all appearances you find there a moral impossibility there, you at least march a part of your army there to become well established in Hesse.[23]

The position at Bielefeld gave the French the advantage of consuming forage from the counties of Ravensberg, Lippe, and part of the principality of Minden, but operations still depended on supplies from Lippstadt and Paderborn. Despite the *Maréchal*'s orders to general officers and *colonels* to leave all their carriages in Münster, with the exception of the *chirurgiens-majors* [surgeons], Chapotte noted that:

> [O]ur army continues to suffer greatly from the scarcity of food; it is very happy with the departure of the troops destined for the army of *Maréchal* de Richelieu and especially the general officers because they hope that, becoming less numerous, they will suffer less;[24] it is astonishing that having the Meuse and the Rhine to bring us food, we are so troubled to get them from the Meuse to the Rhine and from Wesel to us; the roads, it is true, are very bad, but with the abundant wood along the paths of the journey good work should be made good

---

22   Chapotte, *Sous Louis le Bien-Aimé*, p.44.
23   Marquis de Paulmy to d'Estrées, 25 June 1757, in Waddington, *La guerre de Sept ans*, p.415.
24   The princes that left Paris were followed by a train that could not be more excessive: the Duc d'Orléans had an escort of 350 horses, the Prince de Condé of 225 and the Comte de La Marche with 100 horses, and valets in proportion. The army regulated, 'the number of horses that the *maréchaux de France* and *lieutenant-general commandant-en-chef* will have is not fixed. Each *lieutenant-general* will have 30 horses or mules, including those for three carriages; each *maréchal de camp*, 20, including those for two carriages; each *brigadier*, 16, including those for a single carriage. *Colonels* and *mestres de camp* may have the same number of horses without claiming more than their ordinary rations. Lower officers may only have horses and mules according to their rations. There may be a carriage following each cavalry regiment, or each battalion, for the convenience of the officers, and also a single *vivandier*; the other *vivandiers* will only have pack horses. Those of the said *vivandiers* who are not attached to a battalion or regiment will encamp in the King's quarter where the general officers are.' Duc de Luynes, *Memores du duc de Luynes*, Vol.XV, p.253.

HASTENBECK 1757

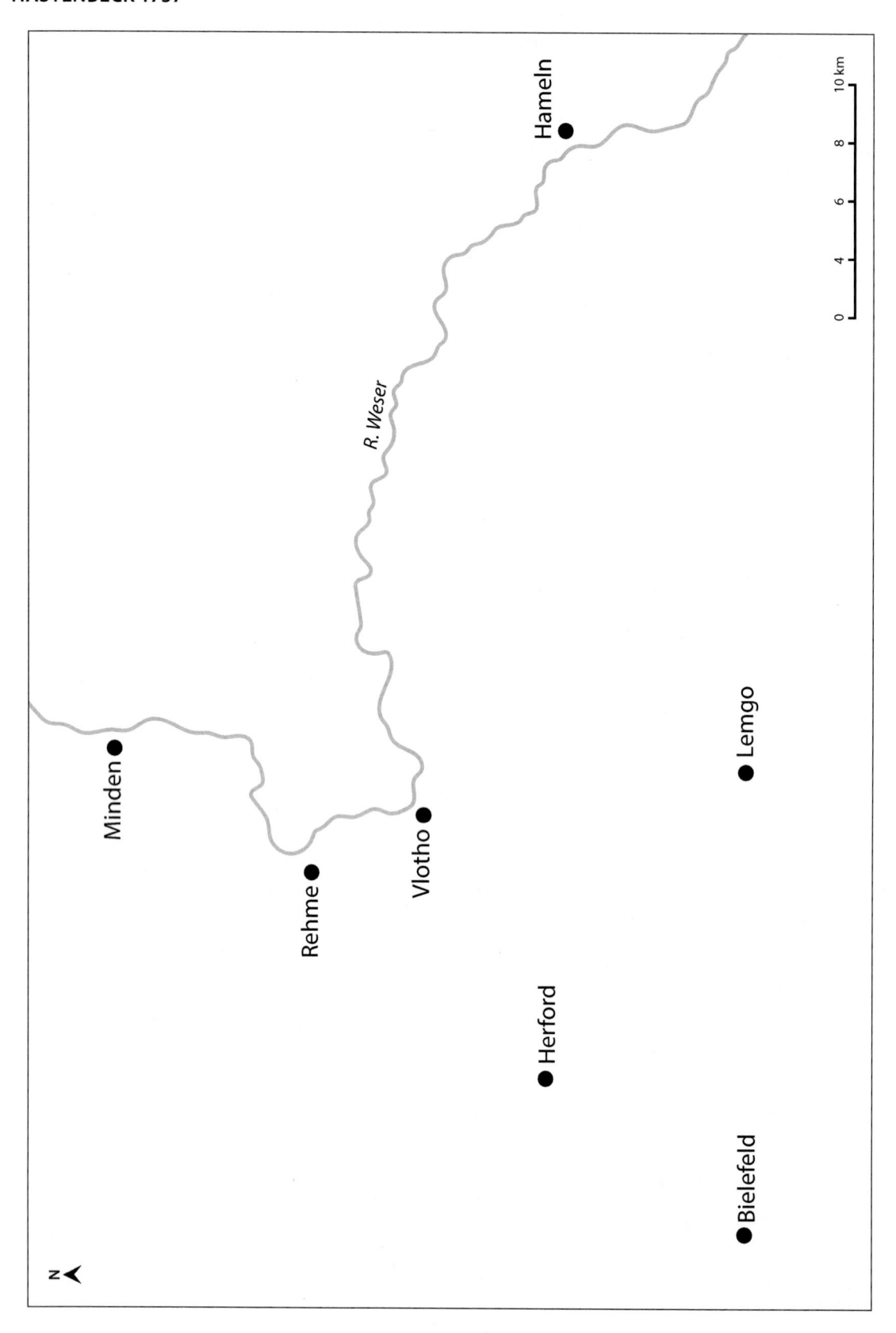

with the labour of 100,000 soldiers, along with many broods of peasants, which should not be long or impossible.[25]

There was no mercy for looters who, if caught in the act by the provost, were hanged in front of the troops. 'There will be four hanged today, the first to be taken; I will send the *capitaine* to prison, and in the event of a recurrence in the same regiment, the same fate will await the corps commander: that is the only remedy that I know of'.[26]

Around 6,000 troops from the Palatinate were expected, who would arrive on the 6th or 7th of July. By the act of 28 March 1757, France guaranteed the Elector Palatine possession of the Duchies of Berg and Juliers in exchange for the occupation of Düsseldorf by a French garrison (at the expense of the King of France) and the dispatch to the French army of these troops.

Twelve squadrons from the Roermond camp by Wesel were also expected to arrive, under the command of the Duc de Ayen, including Chapotte who wrote: 'I left Roermond on 17 [June]; marched through the countryside for three days; stayed in Wesel; four days march to Münster … [the] twelve squadrons that left the Roermond camp will return on the 6th of next month to Brakel … to threaten the Wesel. I believe these detachments will greatly trouble the Duke of Cumberland, it is an excellent manoeuvre that should have been made sooner.'[27]

The two vanguard corps manoeuvred on the wings of the army 100 kilometres from each other, and detachments of light troops appeared unexpectedly and randomly in the intervals so as to keep the enemy permanently mobilised. The Duke of Cumberland finally settled on Minden and Hameln at his storage depot. On June 24, two strong detachments were sent under the orders of the Comte de Bercheny, *lieutenant-général*, 'to support the promenade of the *Maréchal* and the Princes who had gone to reconnoitre the position of the enemy' for the cost of a few skirmishes.[28] The Hanoverian army stretched from Vlotho in the west through the Weser Gorge towards Hameln to the east, protecting the bridges of Vlotho and Rehme. The Prussian corps under the orders of the Prince of Hesse held the right in Minden and another corps on the left in front of Hameln. Detachments stationed along the Weser observed movements along the river.

During this time the Marquis de Dauvet, *maréchal de camp*, had been sent to Ost-Frisia with 1,000 men and arrived in sight of the capital, Emden.[29] Located at the mouth of the Ems, the city was the only seaport held by the

---

25 Chapotte, *Sous Louis le Bien-Aimé*, p.54.
26 *Maréchal* d'Estrées to Marquis de Paulmy, Bielefield 20 June 1757, in Waddington, *La guerre de Sept ans*, p.414. There were around 20 looters in total.
27 Chapotte, *Sous Louis le Bien-Aimé*, p.51.
28 *Maréchal* d'Estrées went with the Duc d'Orléans as well as the Prince de Condé and the Comte de La Marche who served on his staff. SHD, archives du genie, Série 1V, Article 15, Section 1, dossier 5, piece 23. *Journal de la campagne de 1757*. Ladislas Ignace de Bercheny (1689-1778) was from the Hungarian nobility and had come to France in 1712. He had been *inspecteur-général* of the hussars since 1743 and *lieutenant-général* since 1744. He became *maréchal de France* on 15 March 1758.
29 Louis Nicolas Dauvet Desmaret Marquis de Dauvet-Mainneville (1717-1781), *maréchal de camp* from 10 May 1748; *lieutenant-général* in 1761.

King of Prussia who bought it from the Dutch in 1744. The battalion of Cambrésis and the two Régiments de Dragons du Roi and Harcourt marched for 200 kilometres without encountering any resistance. The Marquis de la Chatre, the Comtes de Lillebonne and Scey were sent to scout the state of Emden and were greeted by cannon fire and musketry.[30] The Marquis de Dauvet then made arrangements to storm the town and made use of the only small mortar he had. The next day, 3 July, at 7:00 a.m., the Comte de Lillebonne learned that 70 deserters from the garrison, taken at the outposts by his dragoons, reported great fermentation in the town where the mortar fire had caused horror. Taking advantage of the probable disorder, he sent one of his officers to summon the garrison commander to surrender. Under the pressure of the bourgeois, the capitulation was accepted, and the Comte de Lillebonne took possession of the city gates with 200 dragoons. An hour later, the French detachment entered Emden and the Marquis de Dauvet ratified the capitulation. The garrison of around 500 Prussians were taken as prisoners of war, handed over by the city to guarantee the safety of the French and the full application of the capitulation; many stores were taken as well as several vessels anchored in the port and buildings there. As requested by *Maréchal* d'Estrées, the Marquis de Dauvet was now in a position to raise contributions throughout Ost-Friesland.

---

30   Charles Pierre de Nançay, Marquis de la Chatre, *brigadier* from 1748 and *colonel* of the Régiment de Cambrésis who he led in the 1757 campaign. He became a *maréchal de camp* in 1758 and *lieutenant-général* in 1762. Alexandre Antoine Comte de Scey-Montbéliard (1717-1789), then *mestre de camp* of the Dragons du Roi, he would become a *brigadier* in 1758 and *maréchal de camp* in 1761.

6

On the Other Side of the Weser

The enemy having withdrawn from Bielefeld, the army of the King came to camp there to consume the subsistence of the County of Ravensberg and the Principality of Minden, the Maréchal took advantage of this time of rest to plan his later projects and make all arrangements relating to them.¹

Louis XV was keen for the Armée du Bas Rhin to cross the Weser in the early days of July and send a large detachment to Hesse-Cassel. The King was unaware of the difficulties in carrying out the two operations simultaneously: firstly, the bread ovens under construction at Paderborn could not be completed before 8 July, and it was impossible to go to Hameln without creating an intermediate post within 15 days; secondly, the supply of artillery was not sufficient for the siege of Hameln at the same time as an expedition to Cassel. *Maréchal* d'Estrées chose to invade Hesse which threatened the left of the Duke of Cumberland and opened Franconia to him, allowing communications with the Armée du Haut Rhin led by the Duc de Richelieu, which was assembling around Frankfurt.

In order to conceal his plan as long as possible, the *Maréchal* maintained the pressure on the Duke of Cumberland at Minden on the lower Weser, where the latter had placed most of his troops but still left a considerable body before Hameln. D'Estrées promoted his deception with the corps of the Duc de Broglie in Herford which was reinforced and approached Minden. On 1 July, a second detachment under the orders of M. de Chevert, *lieutenant-général*, advanced with 10 artillery pieces and 20 pontoons on the river as far as Rehme and Vlotho.² A third, commanded by the Marquis de

---

1 Comte de Maillebois, *Memoires du comte de Maillebois* (Amsterdam: Unknown Publisher, 1758), p.6.
2 François de Chevert (1695-1769) came from humble origins and enlisted in the Régiment de Beauce at the age of 11. Made a *lieutenant-colonel* in 1739, he became *brigadier* in 1742, after having distinguished himself in the capture of Prague under *Maréchal* de Saxe, became a *maréchal de camp* in 1744 and *lieutenant-général* in 1748. His corps consisted of the Régiments de Picardie (4 battalions), Vaubécourt (2), Condé (2), Grenadiers Royaux d'Aulan (2); carabiniers (10 squadrons); six 4-pounders, four 8-pounders, 20 pontoons, two engineers and eight men from the Corps Royal de l'artillerie et du génie. The other senior

Souvré, left for Lemgo with 10 pieces of artillery and four work carts.[3] With the enemy thus hemmed in largely on the lower Weser, the river crossing could be undertaken upstream where the corps of the Marquis d'Armentières would go to camp at Erkeln, one kilometre south of Brakel. The rest of the cavalry that had been called up on 28 June from their Münster camp would arrive from elsewhere on the upper Weser, Chapotte recording that:

> I am leaving tomorrow to march until the 6th of next month with one pause; we will stop at Brakel, very near the Weser; we are the last, we are going to be at the head of everything. Our march is very hard, it is difficult in terms of fatigue and in enduring the weather which is very disagreeable.[4]

Believing that he would not be able to take Hameln before 23 July, *Maréchal* d'Estrées chose to act first against the Landgrave of Hesse-Cassel. Under the orders of the Duc d'Orléans, a body of 20,000 men would enter Hesse and would take control of Cassel by 15 July. On the Weser, thanks to the posturing on the Minden side, the reserve of the Marquis d'Armentières would build bridges over the upper part of the river for a future passage, some 50 kilometres south of Hameln. Care would be taken approaching this place not to raise the alarm before time came to begin the siege. The time spent at the Bielefeld camp was put to good use. At a review to celebrate the Austrian victory over the Prussian army at Kolin on the 18 June, *Maréchal* d'Estrées was able to observe his army beautifully turned out. The formations were still at good strength, with squadrons of 140 cavalry and battalions of 575 fusiliers on average (see Appendix II).

The Duc d'Orléans left the camp of Bielefeld on the night of 4 and 5 July with 28 battalions and 32 squadrons, representing about 20,000 men, moving on Cassel via Paderborn, 120 kilometres to the south-east.[5] The expedition was unlikely to encounter strong opposition since the bulk of the Hessian troops were with the Duke of Cumberland. Not wanting to leave the supervision of the crossing to anyone else, *Maréchal* d'Estrées left the Bielefeld camp on 7 July to go to Brakel near the banks of the Weser and the Marquis d'Armentières' reserve. The Comte de Maillebois was left at Bielefeld from where the Comte de Berchemy was to march the rest of the army the next day, 8 July, leading it through Detmold, to Höxter, 70 kilometres further south-east.

---

officers were M. de Montboissier, *lieutenant-général*, and MM. de Poyanne, de la Vallette and de Montmorency, *maréchaux de camp*.

3 This corps consisted of the Régiments de La Marine (4 battalions), la Couronne (2) and Conti (2), the Grenadiers Royaux de Modéne (2), the cavalry brigade of Royal-Pologne; six 4-pounders, four 8-pounders, four work carts and munitions, two engineers and eight men from from the Corps Royal de l'artillerie et du génie. The senior officers were MM. de Souvré and de Morangiés, *lieutenants-généraux*, MM. de Péreuse and Leyde, *maréchaux de camp*. Duc de Luynes, *Memoires du Duc de Luynes*, Vol.XVI, p.98.

4 Chapotte, *Sous Louis le Bien-Aimé*, p.44.

5 Twenty-four cavalry squadrons, one regiment of dragoons, one of hussars and a train of artillery, six *lieutenant-généraux* and eight *maréchaux de camp*.

ON THE OTHER SIDE OF THE WESER

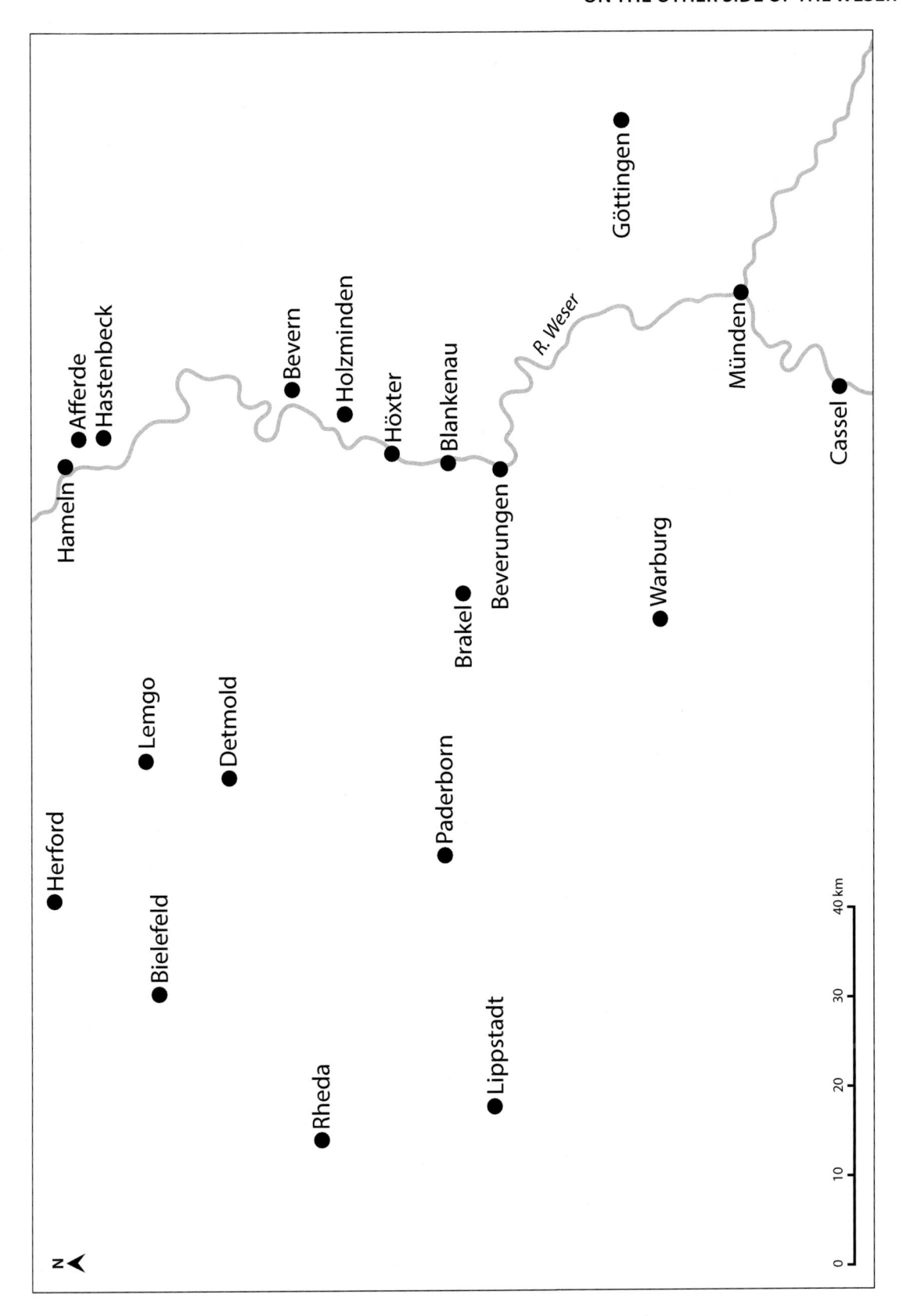

Learning that the Landgrave of Hesse had left Kassel for Hamburg with the Princess, his daughter-in-law, and ordering that the city remain open, *Maréchal* d'Estrées decided to keep the Duc d'Orléans near him above Höxter, occupied by three brigades. On 6 July, at Nieheim, the Duc d'Orléans sent his grenadiers, carabiniers as well as several infantry *piquets* to the Marquis d'Armentières' corps, already 5-6,000 strong, which preceded it by a march. The Marquis de Contades, *lieutenant-général*, was appointed to lead the rest of the advance on Cassel with four infantry brigades and 20 squadrons.[6] At the same time, the Marquis de Péreuse, *maréchal de camp*, was sent with an infantry and a cavalry brigade to march on Münden at the confluence of the Weser and Fulda rivers flowing from Cassel, located 20 kilometres south-west.[7] Münden, a possession of the Elector of Hanover, surrendered on 12 July and its garrison of 400 men taken as prisoners of war. On the 13th, the Marquis de Contades was joined at Warburg by the Grand Equerry of the Landgrave who came to assure him of the country's submission. The Marquis, who had received two hostages as a guarantee of the opening and disarmament of the city, resumed his march to occupy Cassel, which he entered on 15 July without resistance from the militia battalion or dismounted dragoons garrisoned there. The Regent, who brought him the keys to the city, agreed to provide him with all the assistance that the resources of the country could provide; the commandant of the town appealed to him to keep the safety and integrity of the Prince of Hesse's house and gardens. The soldiers of the Hessian militia were sent home and a guard was immediately organized. The Marquis de Contades sent a battalion to garrison Münden and allow the Marquis de Péreuse to leave with Salis's infantry brigade and his cavalry brigade to march on Göttingen, 30 kilometres northeast. Göttingen surrendered on 16 July, at its first summons. Its garrison of about 200 men were taken prisoner of war, eight cast iron and 11 iron artillery pieces were seized with some ammunition. From Cassel, a battalion of the Régiment de Vastan was sent to Marburg, 90 kilometres south-west, to capture the city and thus allow communications with the *Maréchal* Duc de Richelieu's Armée du Haut Rhin when the time came. Leaving 11 battalions and 10 squadrons in different garrisons, the troops of the two expeditions returned through Warburg to join the army at Höxter, which was about to cross the Weser. Hesse-Cassel remained neutral and paid all kinds of contributions without withdrawing its 12,000 men from the British service, which the French would have to fight in the coming days.

On 5 July, the Marquis d'Armentières moved to Lippspringe, five kilometres north of Paderborn, then Driburg on the 6th, and then Erkeln. On the evening of the 7th, he advanced to the upper river with 400 carabineers and 25 companies of grenadiers on the heights of Beverungen,

---

6   Louis Georges Érasme Marquis de Contades (1704-1795), was a *maréchal de camp* in 1740, promoted *lieutenant-général* in 1745. He became a *maréchal de France* in 1758, he would become the *doyen des maréchaux de France* in 1788 and held the last session of the *tribunal de connétablie* in his *hôtel* before its suppression during the Revolution.

7   Charles Prosper Bauyn, Marquis de Péreuse (1710-1776) had been a *maréchal de camp* since 1748 and would be promoted *lieutenant-general* on 15 January 1758 for repulsing a siege and holding out for a month and with little means during the blockade of Harburg.

13 kilometres south of Höxter, to reconnoitre the site of a future bridge. Two hundred infantry and 40 Hanoverian cavalry witnessed the French enter Beverungen and immediately withdrew from the village of Lauenförde, on the opposite bank. The Marquis spent the night in Blankenau. The next day, 8 July, a bridge was safely constructed between four and five in the morning. At noon, the Marquis crossed the Weser with 15 companies of grenadiers and ascended the right bank to Boffzen. In passing, he occupied Fürstenberg Castle, which the enemy had evacuated with such haste that 200 haversacks were abandoned there. Three hundred volunteers scouted up to the villages of Holzminden and Bevern, halfway to Hameln, encountering nothing but a few enemy jägers who retreated into the woods to the east. The detachment returned to settle at Fürstenberg. Having gained a foothold on the right bank, *Maréchal* d'Estrées was able to protect the passage of the Weser. He lodged in Corvey Abbey, a little east of Höxter, in a bend of the left bank of the river. There he awaited the main body of the army and the detachments previously sent to manoeuvre against the enemy on the Minden side. The cavalry was at the Brakel camp at last finding 'a land abundant for fodder … it is cut indiscriminately wherever it is found; this puts the army at ease and restores the perishing cavalry, decreased the hardship, expense, and fatigue of the convoys'.[8]

A few days earlier a staff officer reconnoitring north of Lemgo with a detachment of the Régiment de Champagne advanced on Fort Rinteln on the left bank of the river. Not wanting to leave an enemy position behind, the officer summoned the garrison to surrender, suggesting that he was being followed by a stronger party. The garrison surrendered on the spot and, oddly enough, accepted the order to guard itself until more French troops arrived. On 7 July, during his demonstrations on the lower Weser, the Marquis de Souvré took possession of the fort where he found more artillery than expected. He then continued on his way with his detachment to reach Höxter and join the troops of the Duc d'Orléans. On 8 July, Chevert's detachment went to Horn, 10 kilomstres south-east of Detmold, then went up the Weser towards Corvey Abbey where it camped as guard for *Maréchal* d'Estrées' headquarters. The Duc de Broglie stopped at Bodenwerder, 30 kilomstres downstream from Höxter. An anonymous officer recorded these movements:

> It was on the morning of the 8th that we cast our bridge over the Weser above the village of Blankenau. We got on our horses at ten o'clock and went to Fürstenberg Castle, which is close to Solling Forest. We descended the Weser to Höxter where we crossed the ford. We went from there to Corvey Abbey where there is a very large building and the abbot is a prince of the Empire. We went back to Blankenau to sleep. Today our bridge has moved down between Corvey and Höxter. The Duc d'Orléans came with three brigades to encamp above Höxter; he established his headquarters there. M de Souvré arrived there with his camp. The main army is at Brakel, and M. le *Maréchal* is personally at the Corvey Abbey. So here we are

---

8   Chapotte, *Sous Louis le Bien-Aimé*, p.59.

masters of Hesse; We just have to lay siege to Hameln. When we get take this city, only Bremen and Werden will be left, and we will control this part of the Weser; after which we will not run out of any food. Our winter quarters are safe. You see that everything works for M. le *Maréchal*: he also conducts himself with great caution. On the 13th, the main army will be in the camp at Corvey.[9]

On 8 July, the army corps under the command of the Comte de Bercheny left Bielefeld and the lower Weser, where it had been encamped since 18 June, as described by the Comte de Gisors in a letter to his father:

Without presumption, I dare say that I managed to have the best-marching regiment in the whole army. No officer, under any pretext whatsoever, leaves his division, nor any soldier his rank, without a permission, and, on arrival, they get into line, carry their arms, the banns are published, and the battalions dismissed to their barracks in garrison. As I did not dismount until an hour and a half later, I saw the wood and straw gathering detachments depart myself with the officers who, under my direction, together with armed soldiers form a chain from the canton to the woods. The *piquets* remain under arms, in front of the camp, until everyone has returned. Here are, I believe father, all the precautions one can take regarding discipline.[10]

The troops promised by the Palatine Elector arrived with 39 cannon. The 3rd battalion of the Austrian Prince of the Line regiment and another of the Saxe-Gotha regiment followed from Roermond. The march was slowed by large groups of *équipages* that had been recalled from Münster where they had been left and were blocking the road more than was reasonable, as related by Gisors:

Our march from [Oerlinghausen], which was only three short leagues, lasted nine hours, because of the lack of precision of orders relating to the *équipages*, and of the extreme slowness with which the Palatines march, who perpetually go back and forth. I have adopted the practice of always walking in fours, by which means I never stop, all the paths being able to accommodate this number of men abreast … As for discipline, as for cleanliness, inspection is done on march days like any other; no one is excused from having a fresh que, a curl [of hair] on each side, a well-sewn coat, and soldiers are never allowed to take off their hats on the way. Almost every evening I go to deliver orders, where I try to inspire them with speeches the feelings that the soldiers of Champagne should have. So, half by friendship, half by severity, I try to deliver the phalanx that is entrusted to me.[11]

In a memoir addressed to *Maréchal* d'Estrées, the minister noted the immense number of carriages. 'A *lieutenant-général* and a *colonel* each had 40 with them for ten days. There is no battalion that has more than fifteen. This

---

9   Letter from an unidentified officer, 10 July in Duc de Luynes, *Memoires du duc de Luynes*, Vol. XVI, p.105.
10 Gisors to Belle-Isle, 10 July 1757 in Rousset, *Le comte de Gisors*, p.203.
11 Comte de Gisors in Waddington, *La guerre de Sept Ans*, p.420.

does not prevent us from taking a lot of forage. The *équipages* march unladen and we die like miserable peasants'. To complete the picture, he added 'demands for money and in kind, taxes per day and even violence against the poor inhabitants'.[12] Some counties such as Lippe were almost ruined. To the Count, ally of France and Austria, nothing remained but regrets for his beautiful and abundant harvest and he still had to maintain a contingent of 300 men provided to the Empress from his own income. In addition, the Hanoverian army had not behaved much better in previous weeks; oblivious to the consideration due to their compatriots, Hanoverians, Prussians and Hessians had been marauding over the whole country, where they had looted some villages and devastated crops. The Duke of Cumberland had to crack down, too, and delegate full powers to the provost, who had a pastor with him so as not to delay the hangings. After the successive passage of the two armies, a peasant of the duchies of Münster and Paderborn who kept a horse or cart was very rare. The state of the country was summed up by an unknown French officer:

> The country we travel through from Bielefeld is well cultivated, but produces no wheat; although, we did find some thin and light examples, which suggests the ground is not well suited to it; but rye, barley and oats are of great beauty. It also produces all other species of the same grains abundantly. The country is hilly. There are a lot of woods and wonderful meadows. It makes a good country, but not for those of us who are subsisting in it; there is no bread, wine, beer, or any of the other things necessary for livelihood. The Hanoverians began to exhaust it, and our detachments, which had been at the front for a long time and traversed this whole country, finished destroying it … All sustenance is overpriced. Meat is taxed at 8 *sols* and bread at 4 *sols*; thus these two articles do not vary; but the rest of the produce of the country, is arbitrary. I was sold a pair of small and skinny chickens 4 *livres* 10 *sols*; a pair of pigeons 3 *livres*; an old hare for 10 *livre*. I saw the sale of 4 small turkey poults with the mother for 48 *livres*. Butter, one *livre*, 10 *sols*, and old eggs up to 2 *livres* a *quarteron*. Vegetables are sold in proportion. With such a high cost, it is impossible to have a good table without paying a fortune … there is not enough ordonnance necessary for the daily service of the army.[13]

The army corps from Bielefeld arrived at Corvey Abbey in small stages on the 13th after four days march and one day's rest via Oerlinghausen, Detmold (where it had stayed on the 10th), Horn then Nieheim-Holzhausen, always with the 'road blocked by all the *équipages* ahead of the troops, despite orders so often repeated'.[14] The general officers lodged at Höxter.

On 12 July, the Marquis d'Armentières' reserve had crossed the bridge from Blankenau to Höxter. The Marquis de Souvré and the Duc de Randan had a second bridge established at Corvey, a little to the north, and a third in

---

12 Memorandum of the Marquis de Paulmy to *Maréchal* d'Estrées, received 29 June 1757 in Waddington, *La guerre de Sept Ans*, p.421.
13 Letter of the 11 & 12 July from an unidentified officer in Duc de Luynes, *Memoires du duc de Luynes*, Vol.XVI, pp.106-107.
14 Letter of the Comte de Gisors in Waddington, *La guerre de Sept Ans*, p.420.

the hamlet of Tonenburg a kilometre further north.[15] These two new pontoon bridges led to either side of the village of Lüchtringen two kilometres south of Holzminden:

> We are right on the edge of the Weser ... We found bridges established there; these are apparently ones which were at Blankenau and brought down the Weser. I saw one that is an eighth of a league from here, between Höxter and Corvey Abbey, which is only a good quarter of a league from here; the other is above the town, at about the same distance; it is to serve as communication between the camp we have on this side of the Weser and the one that has been on the other side for a few days ... There are three bridges, each fortified by an advanced work which covers the head, and by a battery of about six pieces of cannon of 16 pound balls. M. d'Armentières with his corps is a quarter of a league in front of these bridges.[16]

Arrangements were made for the army's bread supply using 50 ovens built at Paderborn with the aid of 480 requisitioned carts from the surrounding country.[17] Now the bridges had been put in place, the vanguard was established, and *Maréchal* d'Estrées had made his personal reconnaissance on 15 July, the Armée du Bas Rhin could finally begin to cross the Weser.

---

15 Guy-Michel de Durfort de Lorges, Duc de Randan (1704-1773), elder brother of the Comte de Lorges. He was made Duc de Durfort in 1728 then Duc de Randan in 1733, *maréchal de camp* in 1740, *lieutenant-général* in 1745. He was appointed *maréchal de France* in 1768.

16 Letter from Höxter of 13 & 14 July from an unidentified officer in Duc de Luynes, *Memoires du duc de Luynes*, Vol.XVI, pp.109-110.

17 Four hundred of these were requisitioned in Hesse and 80 were provided by Brunswick, independently of the waggons attached to the food service and the 500 carts from Brabant (as reported to the *munitionnaire* Marquet de Bourgade and the *intendant*, de Lucé, in a memorandum from the *Maréchal*, 17 and 18 July). Louis Charles César Le Tellier, *Maréchal* d'Estrées, *Éclaircissements préséntes au roi* (Paris: Simon, 1758), p.59.

7

Entry Into Saxony

> *M. de Cumberland will come to dispute the entry between the Weser and the Lenne. I intend to attack there as soon as we have prepared the means. I cannot leave to do this before the 19th at the earliest. The country is hilly and difficult, staging posts and provisions have to be prepared but nothing will stop me once this is done. It is apparent that the enemy will take his position in Hastenbeck.*[1]

The Duke of Cumberland had not moved and remained in position at Hameln and Minden.

Frederick's defeat at Kolin deprived him of expected reinforcements but also made likely the recall of the six Prussian battalions attached to Cumberland's force. The Duke had also taken the logical step of advertising his request for the dispatch of a British division, allowing it to be made public in the *Gazette*. The news of the French departure from Bielefeld to Höxter and their vanguard crossing the Weser caused consternation in Cumberland's staff. The movement in Ost-Friesland to the mouth of the river and the move towards Minden had convinced the Hanoverian army that the attack would be made on the lower Weser by turning east towards Minden, cutting off its communication with Hanover. The Duke had even begun evacuating his stores from Hameln to Nienburg, north of Minden. On 10 July, Cumberland began a general movement to cover Hameln. On the 12th, he took up his position along the Weser, to the south-east of Hameln, supported by the mountains. His right was north of the village of Afferde, where he also located the headquarters, one kilometre east of Hameln. His centre was the village of Hastenbeck and his left, towards the south, faced the Hagenohsen woods. The next day Cumberland sent a vanguard of grenadiers to meet the French army as far as Wickensen, 30 kilometres south. As expected, his Prussian battalions were recalled to Magdeburg.

On 16 July, the entire French army marched in six columns from Corvey and began to cross the Weser. Three columns of cavalry crossed at a previously scouted fords and three infantry columns crossed the three bridges. The

---

1   Maréchal d'Estrées, letter to the minister, 16 July 1757 in *Maréchal* d'Estrées, *Éclaircissements preséntes au roi*, p.56

Duc de Chevreuse was stationed at Lüchtringen with four battalions and 12 squadrons while the rest of the army encamped around the headquarters in Holzminden.² A detachment of 800 men was sent east to chase the enemy out of Soling Forest. The success of the expeditions to Hesse and Ost-Frisia, the insistence of the dispatches from Paris, and, perhaps, the suspicion of a secret correspondence between the court and the Comte de Maillebois brought *Maréchal* d'Estrées out of his hesitance. Unusually, he seemed to expect success in his letter to the minister:

> The King's army is finally on the other side of the Weser; D'Armentières is two leagues ahead towards [Holenberg] with his reserve. M. de Cumberland will come to dispute the entry between the Weser and the Lenne. I intend to attack there as soon as we have prepared the means. I cannot leave before the 19th at the earliest. The country is hilly and difficult; marches and provisions must be prepared, but once that is done nothing will stop me … The head of our siege artillery convoy, which had been destined for Cassel, will arrive here the day after tomorrow, and the rest will arrive successively. Everything takes time and patience; I would give myself for few more days, if I were not afraid to give M. de Cumberland time to adapt too well to his position.³

The country between Lenne and Weser was indeed difficult; mountainous and covered with dense forests, often so thick as to leave only small paths. 'All the *aides-maréchaux* are racing to reconnoitre the paths on our right; never has a country been, I believe, less known, nor a project more uncertain than ours', wrote Gisors.⁴ A fellow-officer remarked that 'The paths are extremely difficult to get to Hameln. The Hanoverians are waiting for us there. Our great army will come to Oldendorf; march through Halle to get to Hameln. The roads are very rough and in mountainous country'.⁵

The *Maréchal* planned to march north towards the enemy, along the right bank of the Weser. When the Marquis d'Armentières' vanguard emerged from the defiles of the Lenne, the Duc de Broglie's reserve was at Bodenwerder, on the left bank, and flanked the vanguard by marching in parallel, maintaining communications across the river which was fordable in several places. A third reserve, of two brigades of infantry and two of cavalry, under the orders of the Comte de Randan, would move due east to Einbeck, beyond the mountains, where the road to Göttingen branched to Hameln or Hanover. With the exception of the Comte de Maillebois who, as usual, uttered secret recriminations against his leader's dispositions and was wary of the chances of success, no one on the staff doubted a forthcoming victory.

---

2   Marie Charles Louis d'Albert de Luynes, Duc de Chevreuse (1717-1771). Son of the Duc de Luynes, he was made *maréchal de camp* in 1743 and *lieutenant-général* in 1748. Became *colonel-général des dragons* in 1754. He became Governor of Paris in 1757 then Duc de Luynes on the death of his father in 1758.
3   D'Estrées to Paulmy, Holzminden, 16 July 1757 in Waddington, *La guerre de Sept Ans*, pp.422-423.
4   Comte de Gisors in Rousset, *Le comte de Gisors*, p.206.
5   Letter of an unidentified officer of the Marquis d'Armentiéres' reserve, 17 July 1757 in *Memoires du duc de Luynes*, Vol.XVI, pp.485-486.

ENTRY INTO SAXONY

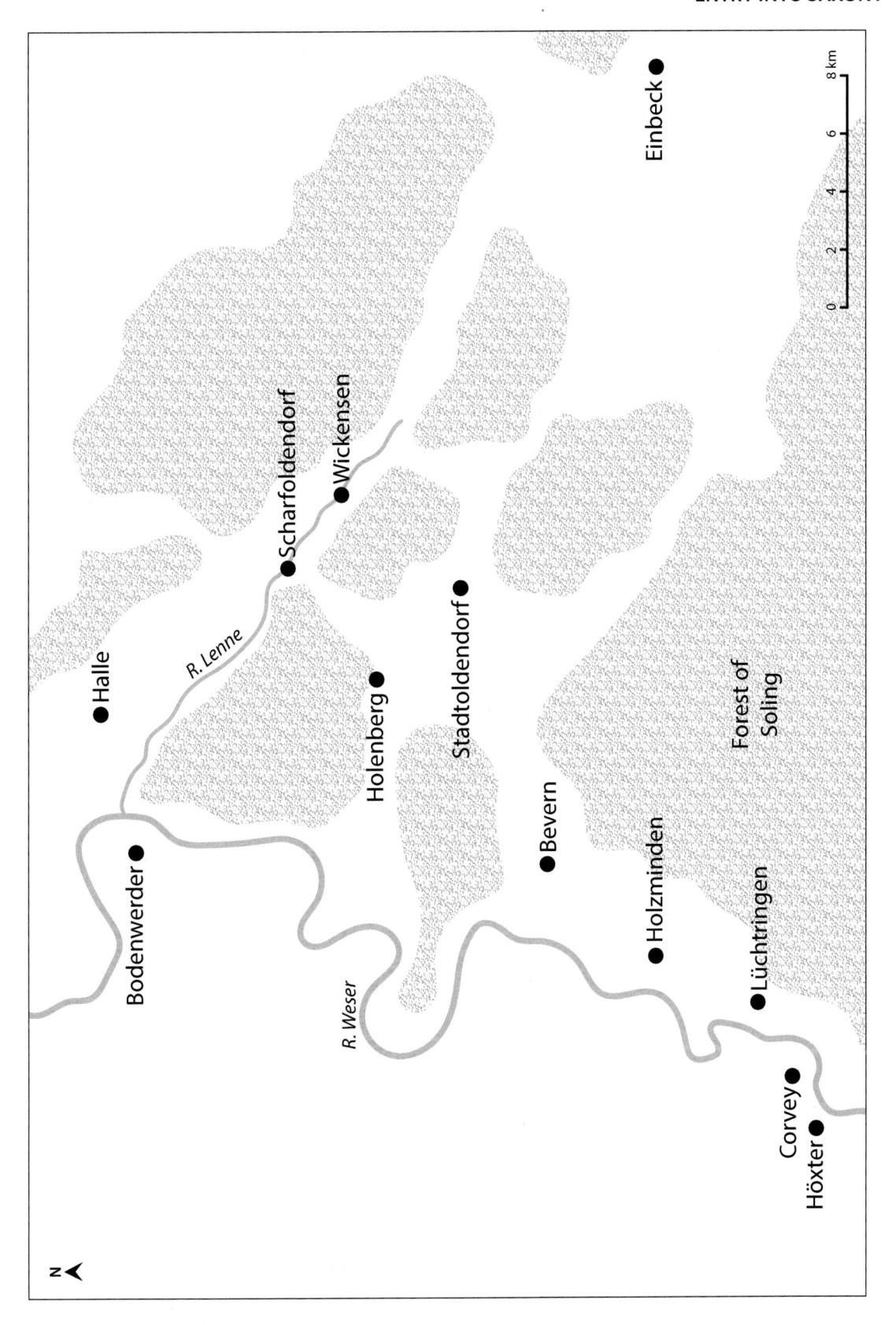

Like the whole army, the Comte de Gisors at the head of the Régiment de Champagne awaited,

> [T]he order to march to a victory that everyone regards as certain, if we dare attempt it. No one is more interested in seizing the opportunity than M. le *Maréchal*; he feels good about it and spoke to me this morning in this tone and is very distressed by the obstacles that the nature of the country presents. However, in my opinion, they must be very strong to balance the advantage that the good constitution of our army gives us over that of the enemy and the ardour with which our soldiers are animated against an enemy that they despise.[6]

The passage of the Weser completed, the next day the Duc de Chevreuse camped at Bevern, a little further north to cover the main camp. On 18 July, he left for Stadtoldendorf 20 kilometres north-east, with the Grenadiers de France and the dragoon regiments d'Orléans, *colonel-général* and *mestre-de-camp-général* to reconnoitre the outlet of the Wickensen gorge.[7]

> The army finally crossed the Weser today. The Duc de Chevreuse again led a column, made up of the Grenadiers de France and three regiments of dragoons, intended to cover the quarters of the Princes all three of whom are here.[8] I believe that tomorrow we will camp ahead of the army … Today we made our second march since crossing the Weser and continue to follow it. We are in country belonging to the Prince of Brunswick-Bevern, brother-in-law of the King of Prussia, and in which he has a poor castle that he lives in … The Duc d'Orléans is staying with him … Only the Princes are here with the same division to cover their quarters as yesterday; the Duc de Chevreuse remains in command of it. The headquarters and the whole army rested yesterday and are still in Holzminden. We are a league ahead, but M. d'Armentières corps is still in front of us, which is about 10,000 men. There is no news that the enemy, who were yesterday still at Grohnde four leagues from here, have decamped, although it was rumoured yesterday that they had made a move. So, if their plan is to wait for us, they will soon be satisfied, because we will still be marching forward tonight or tomorrow.[9]

On the evening of 18 July, the Duke of Cumberland marched with his first line in an attempt to capture the French vanguard. The Hanoverians were advancing south to Halle, where the passage between the mountains and the Weser was narrowest, and a little north of the outlet to the Lenne Valley. Their second line remained below Hameln. The Marquis d'Armentières was at Arholzen, between Bevern and Wickensen, where he defended the two gorges which the enemy could approach him. His outposts, already in contact with the enemy, had lost an officer and four men. On the evening of the 19th,

---

6   Comte de Gisors in Rousset, *Le comte de Gisors*, p.206.
7   Four battalions of grenadiers and three regiments of dragoons of four squadrons each. Du Bois. *Camps topographiques de la campagne de 1757 en Westphalie* (Paris: Veuve Van Duren, 1760) planchet quadruple no.18-21.
8   The Duc d'Orléans as well as the Prince de Condé and the Comte de La Marche, both of whom served on the staff.
9   Unidentified letter from 16 & 17 July in *Memoires du duc de Luynes*, Vol.XVI, pp.113-114.

Chevert went forward with 40 companies of grenadiers, the Grenadiers de France and the Duc de Chevreuse's three regiments of dragoons, to contain the enemy and drive them out of the Wickensen valley to Einbeck. The good positioning of the Marquis d'Armentières and the arrival of reinforcements deprived the enemy of all hope. On the 20th, the Duc d'Orléans, who led a strong detachment from the Holzminden camp to Stadtoldendorf, arrived at the head of four brigades with 12-pounder cannon:

> They camped at Holzminden, a camp which was certainly worse than that of the English at [Dettingen];[10] it was only to be occupied for one night, but they remained there in the greatest security for several days, until, on the 19th, seeing that a detachment of four or five thousand men from the enemy was approaching, they were alarmed to be in so bad a position, but in the manner of a town: the Duc d'Orléans hastily marched with all the grenadiers, dragoons, light troops and cannon; the army was ordered to rest at six o'clock, at ten the order changed: the large waggons were sent back to the Weser and the army marched at three in the morning and took a new camp at Stadtoldendorf without seeing any enemy.[11]

For several days now, the Hanoverian general staff had been looking for the opportunity to separately defeat one of the French divisions and had devised a plan to fall on the Duc de Broglie and cut him off from the rest of the army, but the Duke of Cumberland had refused, working from the defensive opinions of the ministers of Hanover to guard Hameln, and above all the capital. The Hanoverian first line, which had rached Halle on the 18th, and the grenadiers that had been posted to Wickensen and Eschershausen from the 13th, had withdrawn during the night of the 19th to the 20th. Continuing his vanguard mission, the Marquis d'Armentières advanced at Bodenwerder and the whole army encamped between Arholzen and Stadtoldendorf. The day before, the Duc de Randan had returned with his two infantry brigades and 18 squadrons, having attempted nothing against Einbeck, guarded by 1,000 men.

On 21 July, the Volontaires de Flandres, the Volontaires de Hainaut and the Grenadiers Royaux de Solar began the army's march towards Halle. The vanguard of the Marquis d'Armentières arrived before Halle on the 22nd, the Duc de Broglie's reserve was encamped at Grohnde on the opposite bank. Broglie's 14 companies of grenadiers captured the village of Heyen where a skirmish ensued on the morning of the 22nd during a reconnaissance by the Comte de Maillebois on the enemy-held villages of Börry and Frenke. A few cannon shots were exchanged. The whole army left Stadtoldendorf in five columns at 4:00 a.m. and arrived at Halle around 8:00 a.m. where it encamped a kilometre south and east of Halle, where the enemy's first line had been stationed three days earlier. Wooden defences separated the two armies. The Duke of Cumberland had placed outposts at the defences' exits, which were scouted by the Count de Maillebois. The last small enemy posts were pushed back from the surrounding hamlets. 'They are *chasseurs* who

---

10 Where the British army was almost stranded in its camp on 26 June 1743.
11 Chapotte, *Sous Louis le Bien-Aimé*, pp.71-72.

know the country perfectly and who, as soon as they have fired, fall back into the woods with which all these gorges are bordered on both sides.' *Maréchal* d'Estrées arrived early at Halle and was accommodated in the village with the staff. 'The Princes have separate quarters, a quarter of a league from the headquarters, in a hamlet, of only thatched cottages. It is in this hamlet, where there may be around 30 houses, that the three princes, their immense suite and 10 or 12 general officers are lodged'.[12]

Maréchal d'Estrées, in the company of the Princes, then advanced as far as the grand guards of the Marquis d'Armentières. The staff were lodged at the village of Heyen where they took the *Maréchal* to his apartment. From a plateau on the plain north of the village, he sent some volunteers to test the enemy positions at the villages of Frenke and Börry but did not see fit to attack them.[13] At this point, columns of cavalry and then infantry emerged from the wooded heights of Katzenberg which overlooked the two villages:

> Around ten o'clock in the morning, the light troops informed us of the presence of a large body of cavalry, supported by infantry but could not judge their strength because they were marching through the woods with which this country is abundantly covered. *Maréchal* d'Estrées was immediately on horseback and moved forward to reconnoitre the various troops which had been announced to him. On leaving he instructed that the whole camp be ready to take up arms when ordered. The *Maréchal* made his reconnaissance; from a height where he stood, he saw, on a height opposite him, half a league distant, a corps of 2,000 cavalry on a small plain, and saw beyond above, between the two heights, a small combat between our light troops and those of the enemy. When M. le *Maréchal* had mounted his horse, he ordered that the Picardie Brigade come to seize the heights where he was going and that two cavalry brigades put themselves in line and support their right flank. This order was nimbly executed and, as these three brigades reached their destination, the enemy, who saw this manoeuvre clearly without being able to judge our forces because of the peaks and troughs of the country, withdrew their small line of cavalry, and in less than six minutes we saw no one on that height. Our light troops pushed those of the enemies with more force and who, in their turn, assembled on the same height where their small line of cavalry had previously been and held firm there.[14]

Believing he was dealing with the vanguard of a Hanoverian attack, as the light troops skirmished *Maréchal* d'Estrées decided to advance the rest of his army. Staff officers headed back six kilometres to the Halle camp where the tents had just been pitched. It was noon. Officers and soldiers resting after the four-hour march in the morning were raised from their slumbers by the drum roll of *la générale*, as related by Chapotte:

> The troops were hardly at the ground where they were to camp, most of the cavalry had not even dismounted, when a few cannon shots were heard, *la générale* began

---

12 Letter from an unknown officer in Duc de Luynes, *Memoires du duc de Luynes*, Vol.XVI, p.118.
13 Beuvren-Bekhousen and Frinquen according to the maps of the time.
14 Vogüé & Sourd, *Campagnes de Mercoyrol de Beaulieu*, pp.112-113.

ENTRY INTO SAXONY

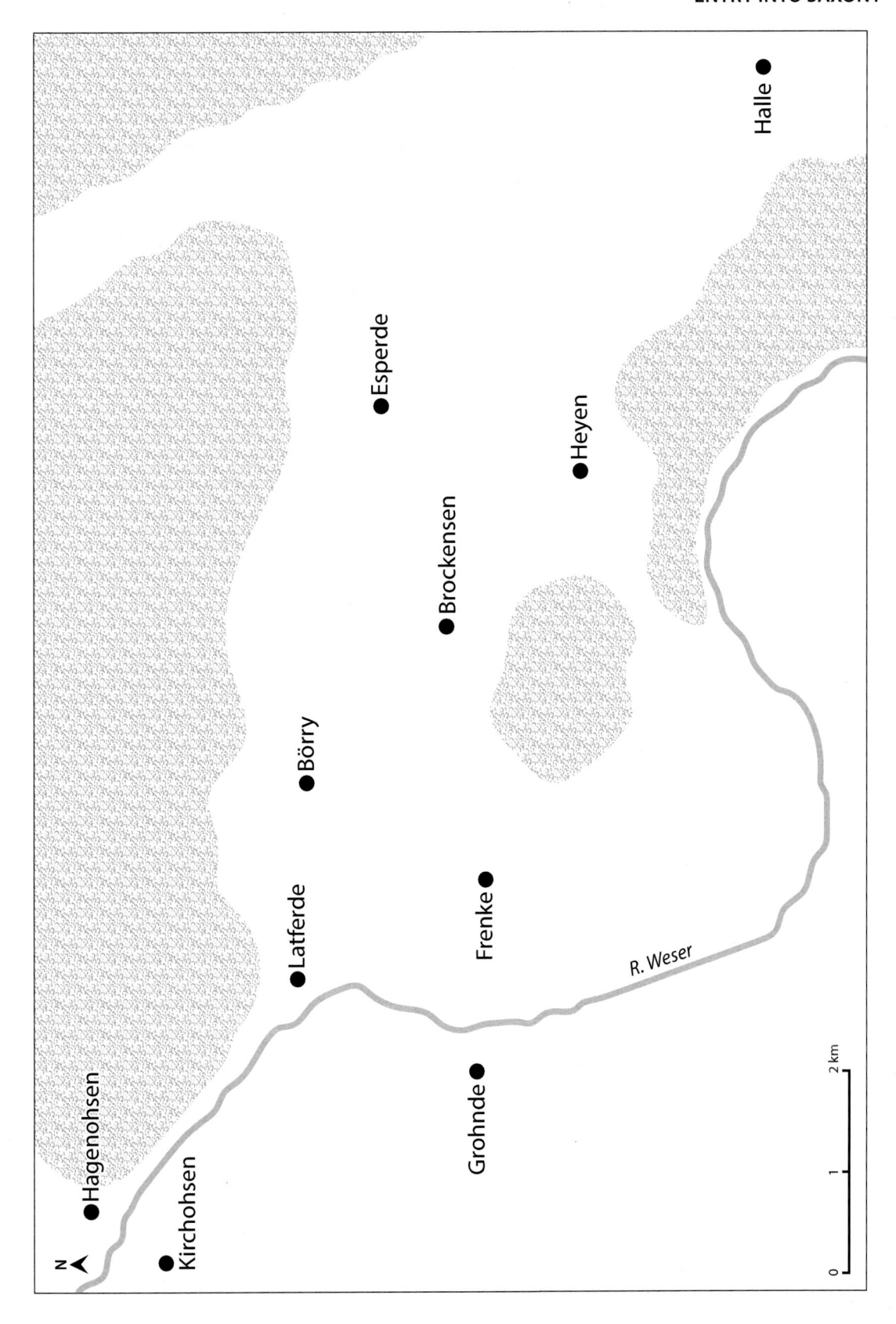

to beat and they were ordered to march. What ardour! What soldiers are the French! Everyone threw their equipment down on the spot wherever he found himself and marched within a minute, and in less time than it would take a traveller to go a league, the whole army travelled half a league from their camp, formed in order of battle without the least confusion and seized the heights and the most advantageous posts. They saw six or seven thousand enemy men moving on the plain; they [the enemy] occupied two large villages there, and it wasn't clear what was in the wooded mountains, where you saw troops coming in and out; their hussars amused us with their skirmishes.[15]

The regiments of the first line assembled and set off in less than three quarters of an hour in good order. Quickly covering the distance, they deployed into order of battle before the second line arrived, which also formed in good order without guides:

The gaiety that ruled the soldier, the words he spoke and the liveliness with which the elders contested for the honour of the first rank moved me to tears; Soon after, Monsieur de Chevert arrived with orders for the second line to take the ground occupied by the first, which had already marched forward. The ranks were never so well observed in exercise as they were in our march; our sickly men had recovered; those who were most weary in the morning tripled their speed, and in spite of myself, the ranks very tight, we kept up the march at the double pace.[16]

The Marquis d'Armentières' vanguard stabilised when the first line arrived. Chapotte noted that 'M. d'Armentières, who rightly dared not venture too far, fired a few cannon shots and in a short time all the ground in front of us was cleared.'[17] Mercorol de Beaulieu explained that:

The officers commanding our troops learned from prisoners they had captured that this thrust of cavalry and the thousand infantry were tasked with a reconnaissance by the Duke of Cumberland and a number of general officers, they informed *Maréchal* d'Estrées and sent these prisoners to him immediately; and they [the French commanding officers], seeing that the enemy was only concerned with withdrawal, made arrangements to attack them on the height. As soon as they began their march, the enemy troops, who were prepared for a speedy retreat, did so with such speed that they only lost about twenty men, most of them wounded by sabre cuts and, as night was ready to fall, the Picardie infantry brigade and the two brigades of cavalry were ordered to return to their camp.[18]

---

15 Chapotte, *Sous Louis le Bien-Aimé*, p.73.
16 Rousset, *Le comte de Gisors*, p.213.
17 Chapotte, *Sous Louis le Bien-Aimé*, p.73.
18 Vogüé & Sourd, *Campagnes de Mercoyrol de Beaulieu*, pp.112-114.

Fusilier of the Régiment du Roi circa 1750-1757. Although a rather naïve artwork from a stylistic perspective, this image gives some useful details of the uniform worn by this unit (including the working dress of the soldiers in the left-background) and of the appearance of a French military camp around the time of the outbreak of the Seven Years War. (NYPL Vinkhuijzen Collection)

Trooper of the Régiment d'Henrichemont Cavalerie. The long coat with lapels was typical of French heavy cavalry regiments, although the base colour of the coat could also be red, blue, or grey. This regiment was stationed in the second line of the left wing at Hastenbeck, as part of the Royal-Pologne Brigade. (Artwork by Patrice Courcelle © Helion and Company 2021)

Dragoon of the Régiment Colonel-Général. French dragoon regiments often fought dismounted as infantry, which was the case with this regiment at Hastenbeck. The uniform is representative of what was worn by this arm of service, although blue was an alternative to red insofar as the colour of the coat was concerned. (Artwork by Patrice Courcelle © Helion and Company 2021)

Light infantryman of the Volontaires du Hainaut. One of a number of all-arms corps employed in vanguard and outpost duties, the Volontaires du Hainaut formed part of Chevert's column on the far right of the French deployment at Hastenbeck. (Artwork by Patrice Courcelle © Helion and Company 2021)

Fusilier of the Régiment de Picardie. The senior regiment in the French line infantry, first of the six *Vieux Corps*, Picardie could trace its heritage back to 1481. Part of Chevert's column at Hastenbeck, the regiment's four battalions were heavily engaged in the attack on the allied left. (Artwork by Patrice Courcelle © Helion and Company 2021)

Grenadier of the Grenadiers de France. When the French army was reduced after the end of the War of the Austrian Succession, the grenadier companies of the disbanded regiments were used to form this new elite unit. Hastenbeck, where it fought on the left wing, was its first battle and it would continue to serve with distinction throughout the Seven Years War. (Artwork by Patrice Courcelle © Helion and Company 2021)

Grenadier of the Régiment de Redding Suisse. Unlike the Grenadiers de France, at the outbreak of the war grenadiers of line regiments wore the same cocked hat as the fusiliers, with only a sabre – rather than the straight-bladed épée of the fusiliers – to distinguish them. Later in the war, bearskins would become more widespread. The red coat and blue smallclothes were common to all Swiss regiments in French service, of which there were two at Hastenbeck – Redding and Salis, brigaded together as part of the reserve. (Artwork by Patrice Courcelle © Helion and Company 2021)

Infantry colours of the Armée du Bas-Rhin. Top-left, Picardie; Top-right, Navarre; Centre-left, Grenadiers de France; Centre-right, Enghien; bottom-left, Salis-Suisse; bottom-right Royal-Suedois. (All images from NYPL Vinkhuijzen Collection)

The whole French army turned back:

> The fatal order to return to our camp arrived. This order was a wound to one and all. To console myself a little, I asked Monsieur de Chevert for permission to go to Monsieur d'Armentières's camp from where the commotion had begun and which was said to be still in contact with the enemy. It was over when I got there. The only benefit of my trip was seeing both sides formations and only resulted in each side withdrawing. All you need to know is that this corps which was assumed to be the enemy vanguard marching towards us is the same corps we had hoped to attack at Halle. Thinking that they [the Hanoverian detachment] were only dealing with a simple detachment of twelve *compagnies* of grenadiers which preceded the camps of the reserve, they thought they could show themselves and when they saw the columns of the army, they quickly withdrew and executed their retreat in good order, because we did not pursue them.[19]

As Chapotte put it, the French 'returned to their camp, piqued and ashamed of having taken such a hot alarm and having shown themselves to be sixty or seventy thousand to remove a body which numbered no more than eight to ten thousand'.[20] Another officer wrote that:

> As we did not know what was behind them in the wood, the *Maréchal* did not see fit to follow them, and after three hours we returned to our camp, as did the Hanoverians, and there is no doubt that as soon as it is dark, they will scamper off in great haste. They were masters of two villages that supported their right and their left; they had artillery in these villages, and they would have had to be forced to fall back on them.[21]

'On the evening that day, it was ordered that the army be ready to march'.[22] The Comte de Gisors wrote: 'Excuse me, my dear father, if I murmur like a soldier to see yet another missed opportunity to fall on the corps of the Hanoverians; when I am more educated, I will surely end up respecting the prudence of generals'.[23]

There was certainly some discontent within the two armies. The Hanoverians had once again missed the opportunity to put an end to the French advance by destroying what they had believed to be only a small scouting body of a dozen infantry companies. The French regretted not having given battle and completely defeating the advancing enemy corps. In fact, determined to wage a full and decisive battle, the *Maréchal* wisely avoided blundering into a partial combat. Justly, and contrary to their tactics of previous days, the Hanoverians had not entirely abandoned their position under cover of darkness, and seemed to want to dispute the ground at a place which favoured them:

---

19 Rousset, *Le comte de Gisors*, p.213.
20 Chapotte, *Sous Louis le Bien-Aimé*, p.73.
21 Letter from an unknown officer in Duc de Luynes, *Memoir du duc de Luynes*, Vol.XVI, p.119.
22 Vogüé & Sourd, *Campagnes de Mercoyrol de Beaulieu*, p.114.
23 Rousset, *Le comte de Gisors*, p.214.

The army, which needed bread, was obliged to remain in the same camp on the 23rd to receive it; during this time the enemy reappeared on the edge of the same woods and in the same villages which they seemed to abandon the day before. M. d'Armentières, who was near them in [Heyen], was often in combat, but without too much commitment.[24]

On the morning of 23 July, the *Maréchal* held a council of war with his *lieutenant-généraux* and announced:

> Gentlemen, I am not assembling you today to ask whether to fight M. de Cumberland and invest Hameln. The honour of the King's arms, his will, his express orders, the interest of the common cause, everything commits us to adopting the strongest resolutions. I am therefore only trying to take advantage of your knowledge and share with you the most appropriate means to attack with advantage.[25]

All, of course, advised to attack. *Maréchal* d'Estrées decided to march against the enemy on the 24th and to fight the next day, 25 July.

Around 9:00 p.m. on the 23rd, according to the *Maréchal*'s orders, the Marquis de Contades left with 30 companies of grenadiers, three regiments of dragoons, and artillery to the village of Brockensen, a short distance from Börry, which the enemy had occupied the day before and continued to hold in force, to act in concert with the vanguard of the Marquis d'Armentières. At the same time, the Marquis de Vogüé would take 14 companies of grenadiers and 600 men of the Volontaires de Flanders and Volontaires de Hainaut to the edge of the woods on the heights of Esperde, on the enemy's left.[26]

At dawn on the 24th, *Maréchal* d'Estrées stepped onto the plateau near Heyen once again to observe the Marquis de Contades' results on his left. On his arrival at around 4:00 a.m., the enemy withdrew their cavalry posts to the rear, west of the villages of Frenke and Börry to Latferde, closest to the Weser; they held the heights of Bückeberg and the woods which bordered this part of the river and which formed an important gorge opening into the plain of Hameln between the villages of Latferde and Hagenohsen where the Duke of Cumberland had his camp. With their forward cavalry pushed back, the Hanoverian infantry finally withdrew from Latferde. The cannon fire from the Marquis de Contades and Armentières, and also the Duc de Broglie from the opposite bank of the Weser, forced the enemy to leave the heights but the Ohsen gorge remained covered by a strong detachment and the woods of the Bückeberg remain filled with infantry. As Chapotte wrote, 'The enemy had their safe retreat and laughed at us; we wanted to probe the woods with the Volontaires, they were strongly repelled'.[27]

---

24 Chapotte, *Sous Louis le Bien-Aimé*, pp.73-74.
25 *Maréchal* d'Estrées, *Éclaircissements présentes au roi*, pp.18-19.
26 Charles François Elzéar de Vogüé (1713-1782), *mestre de camp* of the Régiment d'Anjou Cavalerie in 1736 then the Dauphin-Dragons in 1746. He became *maréchal de camp* from 1748; *inspecteur-général de la cavalerie* and *lieutenant-général* in 1758. He would command the Armée du Bas Rhin in the winter of 1761-1762.
27 Chapotte, *Sous Louis le Bien-Aimé*, p.74.

While the cannon thundered on the left, the Marquis de Vogüé had encountered the first enemy troops on the right, putting them to flight without much resistance. He then took a good position where was able to train his cannon on enemy troops who were previously obscured:

> The noise ceased and was followed shortly after by sharp cannon fire mixed with musketry at intervals: it was the detachment of M. de Vogüé which, still marching through the woods, had emerged onto a plain where he had found the whole enemy army; he stood firm at the opening of the wood which favoured him, he reconnoitred the enemy very well and, after having cannonaded and shot for three hours, he happily withdrew his detachment to the main army.[28]

Mercoyrol de Beaulieu recorded the casualties of the affair:

> In these various attacks we lost about forty men killed and wounded; the loss of the enemy was about the same. We took a few prisoners from them and found that they were from the detachment of the Duke of Cumberland's reconnaissance the day before.[29]

At the Halle camp, the army gathered at two in the morning leaving their baggage behind but did not depart until eight:

> The *équipages* belonging to the different columns followed them. There was a fifth column of artillery. The Duc de Broglie, *lieutenant-général*, with a force of two infantry brigades and some cavalry, continued his march on the left bank following alongside the army which he had done since the main army crossed the Weser. M. le Duc de Randan, marched on the right of the army with two infantry brigades: La Marine and Enghien.[30]

With the French army on the march, the enemy also took up arms. The infantry was stationed in the woods above the Frenke Plain, and the cavalry formed a line behind, facing the Weser between the villages of Hagenohsen and Tündern, two kilometres to the north-west. After succeeding in getting through the woods from the right, the Marquis de Vogüé had discovered the Hanoverian army at the foot of the other slope of the Katzenberg but too close to the woods to prevent a viable route for French deployment.

By late morning *Maréchal* d'Estrées had been informed of the enemy's position and, judging his position acceptable, halted the army's march and set up camp on the spot. The left was at the Weser facing Grohnde, the centre at Frenke, near the plateau, and the right towards the village of Börry (see Appendix III):

> The army travelled about two leagues and encamped, the left at the Weser, the right on heights, supported by very considerable wood … without any kind of

---

28   Chapotte, *Sous Louis le Bien-Aimé*, p.75.
29   Vogüé & Sourd, *Campagnes de Mercoyrol de Beaulieu*, p.115.
30   Vogüé & Sourd, *Campagnes de Mercoyrol de Beaulieu*, p.114.

équipage support ... All the *équipages* had been ordered to march to the left of the army to occupy a large village, located near the Weser, where the mobile hospital was established.[31]

On 24 July around noon, accompanied by a single aide-de-camp, *Maréchal* d'Estrées crossed to the left bank of the Weser by boat to speak with the Duc de Broglie and judge the enemy position for himself, protected by a few troops, whose camp the Duc wrote that he could see 'in its entirety, and the two exit routes they had, one to Hanover and the other to Hameln; I could see the town of Hameln from my windows.'[32] From the point where he landed, looking eastward across the river, the *Maréchal* saw the reverse of the hills occupied by the enemy on his right, as described to him by the Marquis de Vogüé. In front of him, in the background, was the Hastenbeck plain; on the left, the defences of Hameln and in the foreground facing him were the Hanoverian and Hessian cavalry formed along the Weser.

Returning back to Frenke, the *Maréchal* gathered his *lieutenant-généraux* a second time for a council of war around six o'clock. With the exception of the Duc de Broglie and M. de Chevert, the *lieutenant-généraux* and the Comte de Maillebois suggested attempting a turning movement rather than fight. Chevert insisted on a direct attack because 'coming from so far away with a fine army, it was not taking advantage of its daring and goodwill to delay it in front of the enemy, whom we had sought to meet for so long and with so much pain; that delays always irritated the nation.'[33] Some others agree with this opinion and the *Maréchal* postponed his decision until the next day, deciding that 'this moment is of too great importance to take a side so quickly; I will see you tomorrow if you persist in your opinion, then I will ask you the reasons in writing; but I hope I don't need it.'[34] The assembly had barely separated when the Comte de Maillebois went to find the *Maréchal* and persuade him, against the advice he had publicly agreed with, to fight regardless of the advice of the council.

Two curious events took place at this time. The first was reported by the Hanoverian newspaper on 23 July. 'All was quiet when a French courier accompanied by a trumpeter arrived at noon. The French minister at The Hague had learned that the Duke of Cumberland was eagerly seeking *Eau de Luce* [a cologne also used as smelling-salts] and informed the French court. The King of France sent a box of treasure, accompanied by a very pretty letter from the *Maréchal* d'Estrées.' The *Maréchal* gave an account to the Minister of the arrival of a courier with *Eau de Luce* which he passed on to the Duke of Cumberland. The Duke gave one hundred *louis* to the trumpeter, half of which was deducted for the minister's courier.

---

31 Vogüé & Sourd, *Campagnes de Mercoyrol de Beaulieu*, p.115.
32 Duc de Broglie to the minister in Baron Jospeh Duteil, *Une famille militaire au XVIIIe siècle* (Paris: Picard, 1896), p.53.
33 Charles de Mathei Marquis de Valfons, *Souvenirs du marquis de Valfons* (Paris: Émile Paul, 1907), p.264. Valfons was Chevert's *major-général*, chief of staff.
34 *Maréchal* d'Estrées, *Éclaircissements présentés au roi*, p.21.

The second event took place at a chateau on the banks of the river where some French staff officers were dining. Their meal was interrupted by several musket balls shot through the windows of their room. Hanoverian jäger were shooting at them from across the river, but their fire was quickly halted by a general officer. When asked about the officer's identity, locals recognized their master, Graf von Schulenburg, a *generalmajor* in the Hanoverian army, who obviously had good reason to prevent his men from breaking his windows.

On the evening of 24 July, a little after 8:00 p.m., one of the Duc of Broglie's aide-de-camps, who had been watching the enemy's movements over the last three days, saw the beginning of a retreat on the other side of the Weser. He immediately sent a report to the *Maréchal*. By retreating to Hastenbeck, the enemy offered a solution to the council of war although they had only faced an 'advanced body of the enemy, of about six thousand men, commanded by M. de Zastrow, who stopped our vanguard and manoeuvred very well. As we were more prudent than impulsive, he retired after being cannonaded for a while and re-joined the larger part of the army behind him'.[35]

At 1:00 a.m., *Maréchal* d'Estrées gave orders for his troops at dawn. The Duc de Broglie would cross the river by the fords downstream from Hagenohsen, which had already been scouted. Chevert would advance to the heights with the Picardie Brigade and the dragoons, and send the Marquis de Vogüé to resume his position from the day before with the same troops accompanied by the Navarre Brigade. Returning from Einbeck with his two infantry brigades and 18 squadrons, the Duc de Randan would push as far as Bisperode on the road to Hanover, to turn the enemy left.

On 25 July, at 5:00 a.m., the Duc de Broglie's reserve set foot on the right bank of the Weser to reach Hagenohsen where they would join with the light troops and the Belzunce Brigade under the orders of the Count de Mailly, *lieutenant-général*, arriving from Latferde.[36] As Broglie later reported it:

> I sent M. le Comte d'Estourmel, *maréchal de camp*, to the field with 8 companies of grenadiers, 300 Volontaires de Danfernet, 300 volunteers that I was given by M. de La Chaize the elder, a *capitaine* from Poitou, an excellent officer, 200 hussars, 200 cavalry and 200 dragoons with 4 cannons, to precede the reserve which followed very closely. As soon as it was on the march, I followed the detachment and joined it at the Tündern ford, where the volunteers, the grenadiers and the last of the cavalry and dragoons were crossing.
>
> After a few hussars had passed, I went ahead to the village of Tündern and, the fog beginning to dissipate, saw the entire enemy army marching to their right, reaching the village of Afferde, in order to enter the pass leading to Hanover. Another detachment led by M. le *Maréchal* came down from the mountains at the

---

35 Valfons, *Souvenirs du marquis de Valfons*, p.264.
36 Augustin Joseph Comte de Mailly (1707-1794) was promoted as a *maréchal de camp* in 1745, *lieutenant-général* in 1748, *inspecteur-général de la cavalerie et des dragons* in 1749. He was wounded at Rosbach on 5 November 1757 and held prisoner for two years. He was made a *maréchal de France* in 1783 and commanded the troops who defended the Tuileries on 10 August 1792. He was guillotined at Arras on 25 March 1794.

same time. This caused the enemy to halt, and a moment later they marched to their left, and came to a halt at the left of the wood-covered mountains.

The reserve completed the crossing of the Weser at the Tündern ford and the brigades of Poitou and Royal-Suédois threw themselves into the water with great vivacity, although the water was up to their chests.[37]

On the right, Chevert engaged with two brigades in the wooded paths. As the French approached, the Duke of Cumberland withdrew his right wing behind impassable marshes stretching from the Weser to the village of Hastenbeck in the centre, which he torched. He reinforced his left wing with a large battery, of six 12-pounders and six howitzers, protected by foot jäger and his two grenadier battalions from Hesse and Hanover which were placed in the Obensburg woods, south of the Scheckenberg massif. The Duke's front was covered by sunken lanes, with a few squadrons of cavalry left as a precaution at each leg and all the entrances of the defiles were guarded by strong detachments.

Mercoyrol de Beaulieu described the movements of the Picardie and Navarre Brigades:

At daybreak on 25 July, M. de Chevert, *lieutenant-général*, went to the Picardie *brigade* in person; he was given orders to march to a junction with the Navarre Brigade; but, being farther away than Picardie, Navarre probably needed more time, as it was encamped to the right of the second line … The Navarre Brigade, which was to join us, had not appeared so M. de Chevert decided to send them an aide-de-camp, to direct them to the meeting point indicated to him. Picardie set off, its four guns at its head, with no other crew than the mounted servants. After covering three quarters of a league over the plain it climbed a rather steep height, the summit covered with wood. This height was as the others, no higher, but formed a forest half a league wide, fairly clear and all of tall trees. We put light troops in front and on the flanks because we had no horseman. Our march was made with great security, which became so widespread and assured that the enemy were far from risking a battle; and General Chevert was certain of the opinion that the enemy's army was heading for Hanover, and all the officers, away from the generals, privately joke that they were reminded of the certainty that our generals had had that the allies would not be waiting for us at Ans and Raucoux.[38] So talking, we crossed the forest; a very dense fog covered the horizon, so the edge of the wood where we stood appeared before us like a lake of water or darkness.

The sun, already high (the time being seven to eight o'clock), soon allowed us to discover a hillock covered with wood and troops whose gleaming bayonets revealed them to us; for the same reason they saw the head of our column. M. de Chevert ordered to form line, which was carried out. During this manoeuvre we saw agitation and movement in the enemy troops, who extended their left. This indication from them led General Chevert to believe that they were not in force and possibly on the move to withdraw by the Hanover road, which was a quarter

---

37 Broglie to the Minister, in Duteil, *Une famille militaire au XVIIIe siècle*, pp.55-56.
38 Where *Maréchal* de Saxe had to launch three successive assaults before victory on 11 October 1746.

of a league from the position they occupied. Every moment the fog left the heights and seemed to thicken over the plain. M. de Chevert ordered the brigade march ahead to seize the hedgerows about seven or eight hundred paces from the edge of the wood about halfway to the enemies. The regiment arrived at these hedges in line. M. de Chevert, whose project was to march forward to the height held by the enemy in order to attack them there, continued to think this was only a rearguard of their army and ordered all the soldiers who had axes or billhooks to cut through the hedges. As they were doing this, M. de Lusignan,[39] *capitaine* of the regiment, commanding the four 4pdr guns attached to the *brigade*, said to M. de Bréhant: "The enemy troops in front of us are within reach for us to inconvenience them; Besides, we will learn if they want to answer us and if they have cannon, and that may help M. de Chevert know what he is dealing with. This proposal being to M. de Bréhant's taste, went immediately to join M. de Chevert, near the centre of the regiment observing the hedge cutting. M. de Chevert examined the enemy position, who at this moment appeared to be a line of three or four battalions. The fog was slowly rolling in. The General approved. M. de Bréhant returned to M. de Lusignan, who was ordered to open fire. M. de Lusignan, in the meantime, had arranged everything; the gunners were at their guns. When the order was given, the fire began, which caused confusion and great agitation to the battalions which received the shots. After a six-minute fire, the enemies retaliated with a battery of six cannon, the balls of which were nearly double [the weight] of our own.

At this instant the Navarre Brigade arrived. M. de Chevert told them to come and line up on our left, which they did. As it crossed the small plain, between the wood and the Picardie Brigade, the enemy's cannon killed or wounded some fifteen soldiers. By this time it was nine o'clock in the morning; the fog cleared … and we found the entire enemy army drawn up in line. From their second line, moving within reach of the troops on their left, a second battery of eight guns was being directed against the two isolated Brigades of Picardie and Navarre.

About fifteen riders from our light troops, alerted by the noise of the cannon, told General Chevert that the whole French army was on the march, the General being informed, enquired about the distance, to which they replied, an uncertain account. He then gave the order to the *maréchal des logis* who commanded to go with his troops to reconnoitre the progress of our army and report to him; he added one of his aides-de-camp. Seeing that he was no longer dealing with a rear guard but with the whole army, he ordered that the two brigades under his command should, march back across the small plain which separated them from the woods with a right about face, enter the woods, take cover from the cannon and, with another right about face, face the enemies. This order was carried out without much loss, as the enemy cannonade was misdirected.

The General … went to the left flank to look for the army and see if it would arrive, but in vain and he could not see anyone. If the enemy had known our position well, they could have taken great advantage of it, for, after having overthrown these two brigades, they would have found themselves on the right flank of the King's army and the inconveniences which may have followed would

---

39   René Honoré Couhé de Lusignan was born at Saint-Pierre-de-Maillé (Vienne) in 1724. He volunteered as a *lieutenant* in 1745, became a *capitaine* in 1755, and became *major* of the Régiment de Brest in 1777.

have been very unfortunate. It was only after four hours stationed in the woods that we discovered the other columns of the King's army, one of which on the right came to press on the right of the wood where we were. Our small morning cannonade had accelerated the departure and march of the army.[40]

Maréchal d'Estrées had moved to the left, towards the Weser early in the morning. The fog had thwarted the reconnaissance and it was after eight o'clock when he ordered the army to break camp. Chapotte related that:

> The sound of the cannon was heard by our detachments that had been prepared in the night, which pierced the mountains and woods on all sides and descended onto the plain where the Duke of Cumberland's army was arrayed; but we did not believe it and we did not want to see it; it was certain that they had withdrawn and that it was only the rear-guard[41]

The army did not arrive on the heights of Hagenohsen until 4:00 p.m. due to difficulty of passing the narrow defiles. Since attacking in the centre did not seem possible, the *Maréchal* decided to take control of the heights on his right. Already well advanced, Chevert was in charge of the manoeuvre with his two brigades of Picardie and Navarre and was reinforced by the Brigade La Marine. Mercoyrol de Beaulieu picks up the story again:

> At two o'clock in the afternoon, M. de Vallière arrived, *lieutenant-général* in command of the artillery;[42] after a short conversation with M. de Chevert, he dismounted, walked in front of the wood, asking to be alone so as not to attract unnecessary fire on the curious (which had already happened, when three or four had gone out together, causing the loss of four soldiers killed in the wood). M. de Vallière made his reconnaissance and observation quietly on the whole battle front held by the enemies; he went into the woods, taking glasses and, from a tree on which he leant, spotted several batteries, as we had already done, at the bottom of the heights where their left appeared to be holding the summit, we discovered a very low-angled redoubt. As for the rest of their order of battle, I have spoken of this above but to reiterate: the right towards Hameln; a grove on the plain they occupied was within cannon shot of Hameln; their lines were backed by woods which extended to the heights against which their left was supported; ahead and close to the left was the village of Hastenbeck; the summit of the mountain was lined with troops, those which we had discovered in the morning that we had cannonaded ourselves; one of their batteries were established halfway up the height and the other at the bottom of the mountain, which deserved the name due to its great elevation and is covered with woods with coppiced parts where

---

40   Vogüe & Sourd, *Campagnes de Mercoyrol de Beaulieu*, pp.115-116, 120-125.
41   Chapotte, *Sous Louis le Bien-Aimé*, p.75.
42   Jean Florent de Vallière, (1667-1759), born in Paris (Seine), became a *cadet* in the artillery in 1688, became *maréchal de camp* in 1719, *directeur-général de l'artillerie* in 1720, he was the author of the 1732 artillery regulations which standardised the calibres used within the French artillery. He became a *lieutenant-général* in 1734.

only a lone man could only penetrate with great difficulty, which we experienced the next day.

M. de Vallière remounted his horse and went to confer with *Maréchal* d'Estrées on what to do with his observations. An hour later he arrived back, followed by an artillery train of twenty-five pieces of 12- and 16-pounder guns, and four of 24; he designated and ordered their location. All of this was done without the enemies firing a cannon; we saw that they were busy placing their own. All the artillery horses were brought into the woods, a few wagons were left scattered on the plain, which held the cartridges for the service of the artillery.

M. de Chevert, could see that the wood where we were was going to be the drain of balls from the cannonade which was being arranged, the two brigades under his orders were sent to go eighty or one hundred paces into the wood and take cover, and when this order was executed, the cannonade began; it was a terrible uproar, both from us and our enemies; the number of guns was equal on both sides, but whether our batteries were better placed, our gunners more skilful, or the position of the sun more favourable, coming from behind us and shining the eyes of the enemy, we saw them abandon their pieces as time went on. Ours made mischief by decreasing their fire, only to increase it again when they returned, and at the moment the unfortunates reached to their guns, they were driven away in a cruel manner. Most of their guns were destroyed; they lost a considerable number of their gunners, and by half past seven in the evening their fire was extinguished. This cannonade, which started at four o'clock in the afternoon, caused great damage to their lines, where they lost many horses and men.

As for our losses, there were four gunners and M. de Chevert's horse, killed in the wood. Truly a terror had taken hold of the enemy gunners that, aiming extremely badly, all their balls passed over the heads of our gunners and struck the tops of the trees in the wood where we were. Our batteries continued to fire on those of the enemies which they had abandoned, to destroy them as much as possible, and the fire lasted as long as the rest of the day, they only had the courage to try to move them to safety and waited until night to provide for it. After the battle, we were informed that in this cannonade they lost a hundred artillerymen.

The cannonade ended, there was curiosity about the effect of the guns, and everyone thought of having a bite to eat, for most of the officers hardly had more than a piece of bread all day, and I was one of them. This was done speedily, I joined M. de Bréhant, who was at table on the grass with General Chevert, who had just arrived from the *Maréchal* d'Estrées. Their meal taken (it was then a quarter past nine), M. de Chevert ordered the two brigades under his command to be ready to march.[43]

The heights on the left and on the right were held, the army bivouacked in several lines with the cavalry behind, on the left, while the *Maréchal* worked out a new plan of attack for the next day.

---

43 Vogüé & Sourd, *Campagnes de Mercoyrol de Beaulieu*, pp.125-128.

8

Plan of Attack – 26 July

I accompanied M. de Chevert to the Maréchal who … gave him a description of the terrain crossed by the hussars, the plateau where Bussy had been, and assured him that the enemy left could be turned and would be beaten if they were flushed out from the heights dominating the centre and the right of their army.[1]

The right bank of the Weser is bordered by mountains which often extend to its banks and are sometimes a few kilometres away. By withdrawing his first line from Hastenbeck, the Duke of Cumberland had chosen his battlefield to be on the spot of his former camp. It was a small plain four kilometres wide, from the wooded slopes of the Scheckenberg massif to the east, to the banks of the Weser to the west. There were rye fields at the foothills of the mountain which descended to a small stream which flowed northwest from the village of Voremberg to Hastenbeck. The plain then opened onto a vast meadow which became very marshy towards the river where the stream emptied. The Duke of Cumberland found many advantages for a defensive position to compensate for his numerical inferiority.

From the heights of Bückeberg (At the top of the foothills above Hagenohsen), looking north-east, with one's back to the river, one can view all of the Hastenbeck plain. It was here that *Maréchal* d'Estrées made his reconnaissance on the 25 July and where he positioned himself when battle took place the next day, in the shade of a lime tree.[2]

Behind him, the Weser flowed north and was fordable in several places scouted by the Duc de Broglie, linking Kirchenohsen and Emmern on the left bank to Hagenohsen on the right. The town of Hameln, to the left in the distance and downstream was 'a modern fortified place of good curtain walls, with linked bastions and *demi-lunes*, a covered way and clad with good masonry'.[3] Between the bastions of this small fortress were the villages of Tündern and Hagenohsen, along the Weser, were marshy meadows

---

1 Valfons, *Souvenirs du marquis de Valfons*, p.267.
2 The following description of terrain borrow extensively from the remarkable work of Richard Waddington.
3 Vogüé & Sourd, *Campagnes de Mercoyrol de Beaulieu*, p.114.

divided by so-called Tünder-Anger hedges and a few crops. Beyond the marsh, rising east was a weak escarpment known as Sintelberg, to which the Haste stream, lined on each side by willow trees, served as a natural ditch. Towards the far right, almost hidden by (these foothills), was the village of Afferde, headquarters of the Duke of Cumberland. Opposite the *Maréchal* in the valley of the stream were the Hastenbeck orchards. On the immediate outskirts of the village near the last crops was where the gentle slope of the Schmiedebrink began beyond the stream, which flowed from the wooded foothills of the Scheckenberg massif which filled the entire right of the panorama, around six kilometres away. At the south eastern side of the mountain was the summit of Obensburg with its high grove of oaks and beeches which dominated the villages of Hastenbeck and Voremberg. From the last houses of Voremberg to the east, two deep ravines lead to the top of the Obensburg which rose steeply through the forest. Finally, on the far right a pass connected the village of Voremberg, on the southern slope of the Scheckenberg mountain, to Völkerhausen on the wooded hill of Katzenberg, an eastern extension of the Bückeberg.

The Army of Observation had 40,000 men at its disposal, from Hanover, Hesse, Brunswick, Saxe-Gotha and Lippe. Morale was still good and the men ready to fight. Protected by the Tünder-Anger swamp and ponds, the Duke of Cumberland left just two battalions, four squadrons and his mounted jäger to guard his communications across the bridge over the Hamel into Hameln. He then arranged 20 battalions and 22 Hanoverian squadrons to his right, on the Sintelberg. In the centre, 11 squadrons and 11 battalions of Hessians plus four of grenadiers in a second line occupying the north of a ravine behind the village of Hastenbeck to the edge of the thickets at the bottom of Scheckenberg. The wooded and rocky slopes of this mountain offered protection, which was quite steep on the western face, nevertheless they had to hold firm or risk turning the entire line. On the left were seven Brunswick battalions, two of grenadiers from Hesse and Hanover and the foot jäger. There were six squadrons and three Hanoverian battalions as a reserve at Afferde. The Duke made up for his low numbers by giving the enemy a narrow approach, just one kilometre wide. This was between Hastenbeck and the Scheckenberg and protected by three batteries. One on the left and furthest east, on the foothills of the mountain, would pour fire on the flank of the attacking columns with its two 12-pounders, two 6-pounders and two howitzers. The second was in a redoubt below in the valley rising to the Obensburg and was a larger battery of eight 12-pounders and four howitzers. The third battery was further west, on the Schmiedebrink, and would prevent an advance past Hastenbeck, now cleared of troops, using six 12-pounders and four 6-pounders sent from Hameln. The Hanoverians were quite confident:

> Our front was narrow and extremely strong, due to the village of Hastenbeck, which the enemies had to pass, and a very deep sunken road between us and the village, the communications of which had been severed after we left our camp there. Our right was on a height in front of which there were marshes, or rather a few streams. The slope from this height was so steep that it looked like a purpose-

built bulwark, so that we had nothing to fear from any artillery that might have come from a distance. It could not be flanked, as it curved towards Hameln's cannon, and the detours that this height forced seemed to be on purpose so that our batteries, stationed in the dips, could fire on their flanks. In short, it was unassailable, and the Tünder-Anger, which was in front, could only be what it was, that is to say, a theatre for the races and skirmishes of the hussars. The left wing ... commanded the whole village from the height where it was stationed. Everything was dense thicket woods, and on the side there were steep heights and ravines that looked more like precipices. It did not appear probable to form an attack there with artillery and, for safety, an abattis was ordered there which was constructed during the night, as well as the batteries. Bisperode's post had been manned the day before with four hundred infantry and this post was quite interesting; it was entirely on our left, a quarter of a league from our wing, commanding the great passage [that is, the road to Hanover], and having a good ditch could only be taken by cannon. All these circumstances made us see our position as very strong, and not without reason.[4]

On the French side, the Armée du Bas Rhin had lost a good part of its force since crossing the Weser; some had been sent to the Upper Rhine with the Prince de Soubise, others were sick in hospitals or left behind securing various communications and supply posts. *Maréchal* d'Estrées still had 84 battalions, 10 of which were Palatine and four Austrian, plus 53 squadrons. This totalled around 48,000 infantry and artillery under arms and 7,000 cavalry. The army retained its enthusiasm and were eager to finally face an enemy who had never ceased to retreat.

As soon as he saw the Hanoverian positions, *Maréchal* d'Estrées noted that their right was unapproachable. The centre, behind Hastenbeck on the Schmiedebrink, defended by the three batteries and protected by good fascines and gabions, could only be attacked after capturing the heights of Scheckenberg on the extreme left of the enemy. On 24 July the Marquis de Vogüé deployed on the Katzenberg; he was joined by Chevert on the 25th, and together advanced in front of the southern foothills of the Scheckenberg where he was cannonaded from both sides. By the end of the afternoon, Chevert was

> [V]ery upset to return to the army leaving such a useful post for our overall position. We had to obey; but he had, like a good soldier, made the most of his time while awaiting word from the general. M. de Bussy ... was posted in the woods, on our right, with two hundred volunteers;[5] this officer, as intelligent as he was brave, and who spared nothing to be educated, gave a hussar twenty louis from his own pocket and promised him fifty on his return if he would skirt around the enemy and go to reconnoitre the ground to their left, and that, if he was captured, he would call himself a deserter and do his best to escape: The hussar succeeded beyond all that could be hoped for; he went everywhere, saw

---

4   'Hanoverian Journal', cited in Rousset, *Le comte de Gisors*, pp.219-220.
5   Jacques Joseph Bouchard Patissier de Bussy was the 32-year-old younger brother of the future governor of India. He was a *lieutenant-colonel* and was killed during the Battle of Hastenbeck.

all, did not meet anyone and gave an exact account of everything, which would be very useful to us the next day. Our detachment returned on the 25th at six in the evening. M. de Chevert, whom I was accompanying, reported to the *Maréchal* and expressed regret at not having been able, by his order, to maintain a favourable position. He gave him a description of the terrain which the hussar had traversed, and of a plateau where de Bussy had been, assuring him that the enemy left could be turned there, and that they could beat them if they were flushed out from the heights which dominated the centre and the right of their army. The same unspoken reason for the remoteness of the bread convoy remained. The *Maréchal* pretended not to agree with Chevert, who, very angry, returned to his division, very close to the post occupied by the *Maréchal*. Around seven in the evening the *Maréchal* learned that the [bread] convoy was only a league away, which determined him to send for M. de Chevert to discuss his project.'[6]

On 25 July, around 7:00 p.m., the *Maréchal* assembled his *lieutenant-généraux* for the third time for a council of war at his headquarters in the forest, patrolled by sentries. Despite the difficulty of the enterprise, the *Maréchal* was determined to make efforts on his right by attempting to climb the mountain range from the east and so bypass and encircle the enemy left. Initially he intended that the Duc de Randan's reserve would perform this task and advance on the road to Hanover but in the end he gave it to Chevert who was already forward and had reconnoitred the start of the route.

The *Maréchal* subsequently explained his disposition to his King:

> M. de Chevert ... asked me for five brigades. As I still intended twenty-two battalions under the orders of M. d'Armentières, to support this attack as a diversion, I found that it was putting too great a force in the woods, and I insisted on giving only three or four brigades. The good opinion I have always had of Mr. de Chevert, his reputation, his courage was too well known to me not to designate this particular corps to him.[7]

Chevert ended up with the Volontaires de Hainaut and Flandres and 12 battalions; eight from the Picardie and Navarre brigades, as the day before, plus the four battalions of La Marine, initially intended for the Marquis d'Armentières.

The Marquis d'Armentières, with the Alsace, Belzunce and Couronne brigades plus the two Austrian battalions, would march by the edge of the woods that Chevert's column would have to skirt and then go through, and would support with a head-on attack against the enemy's left wing and its great redoubt. He would be supported by the Duc de Chevreuse with three regiments of dismounted dragoons.

The Marquis de Contades with 10 battalions and the Comte de Guerchy, *lieutenant-général*, with the grenadiers, would attack the centre between the

---

6 Valfons, *Souvenirs du marquis de Valfons*, pp.266-267.
7 *Maréchal* d'Estrées, *Éclaircissements présentés au roi*, p.20.

HASTENBECK 1757

French general officer circa 1757. (NYPL Vinkhuijzen Collection)

village of Hastenbeck and the woods of Scheckenberg.⁸ The Duc de Broglie would hold the left with his reserve and, moving to the left of the village, would then act against the enemy posted on the Schmiedebrink. These three would not begin their movement on Hastenbeck until the right wing had progressed sufficiently to turn the enemy left.

The Marquis de Souvré would hold the far left in the second line with the Palatine troops of *Generalleutnant* Baron von Isselbach. The Duc de Randan would hold the far right, in the second line, in the Voremberg Gap opposite Bisperode, on the Hanover road, with the four battalions of the Brigade d'Eu.

The Marquis d'Anlézy, *lieutenant-général*, would remain in reserve at the foot of Katzenberg, with the eight battalions of Champagne and the Swiss Reding Brigade.⁹ The artillery of M. de Vallière, *lieutenant-général*, and the Chevalier de Fontenay, *maréchal de camp*, would be distributed over the entire battle front.¹⁰ Finally the cavalry, without any favourable ground for action, would remain placed under the orders of the Duc de Fitzjames, *lieutenant-général*, and the Marquis de Poyanne, *maréchal de camp*, behind the infantry columns which they would follow as closely as possible to respond to their needs.¹¹

On 25 July at around 9:00 p.m., Chevert began his movements to launch his attack the next morning as agreed and flank the enemy's left: The two brigades of Picardie and Navarre made their arrangements while that of La Marine joined them. The Volontaires were sent forward around 10:00 p.m. The march began around 11.00 p.m., as related by the Marquis de Valfons:

> Under cover of night, we set out, guided by Rome, *lieutenant-colonel,* of the Légion de Hainaut, who had scouted the ground. The twelve *compagnies* of grenadiers formed the head [of the column]; then came four cannons, the four battalions of Picardie, four of Navarre and then four of La Marine. We went to the village of [Voremberg], from where, turning right, we defiled by sunken lanes through the woods occupied by the enemy, within musket range of their patrols, who continually fired a few shots to warn of our march; it was accomplished as desired, despite the greatest difficulties. I was very worried: having finished putting the Régiment de Picardie into line, I expected to find the Régiment de Navarre next;

---

8   Claude Louis François Régnier comte de Guerchy (1715-1767). Promoted *maréchal de camp* in 1744 and *lieutenant-général* in 1748. He was the French ambassador to London between 1763 and 1767.

9   Louis François Damas, Marquis d'Anlézy (1698-1763). Promoted *maréchal de camp* in 1743 and *lieutenant-général* in 1748.

10 Louis Charles Claude Andrey Comte de Fontenay (1696-1774). Promoted *maréchal de camp* in 1748, went on to succeed M. de Vallière as *Inspecteur général du Corps Royal de l'artillerie* and was promoted *lieutenant-général* in 1759.

11 Jean-Charles de Berwick, Duc de Fitzjames (1712-1787), son of *Maréchal* Berwick and grandson of the King James II of England. He had been *mestre-de-camp* of a cavalry regiment since 1733 and served alongside his father at the siege of Philippsbourg in 1734 who was shot dead while inspecting the trench, covering his son with his blood and brains. He was promoted to *maréchal de camp* in 1744, *lieutenant-général* in 1748; he would become a *maréchal de France* in 1775. Charles-Léonard de Baylenx, Marquis de Poyanne (1718-1781). Promoted to *maréchal de camp* in 1748, second in command of the carabiniers, became a *lieutenant-général* and *mestre-de-camp des carabiniers* in 1758.

but, confused at the turn at the village of [Voremberg], they had followed the straight path. I ran alone, on foot, in complete darkness, at the risk of falling into some patrol, and was fortunate enough to find the regiment, whose leader was already in reach of the enemy's first guards; I had them move back and put them in line with the Régiment de La Marine, to the left of Picardie; everyone had arrived by two o'clock in the morning on the plateau reconnoitred the day before by MM. de Bussy and Vioménil, aide-de-camp to M. de Chevert.[12] Beyond M. de Chevert's camp, four hundred men from the légions de Hainaut and Flandres, commanded by La Morlière,[13] hid in the woods occupied by the enemies to our left; Bussy and the two hundred Volontaires guarded the edge of the wood ahead of our front, where the two hundred horse from the two légions were stationed on a small plain, commanded by M. de Bourgmary.[14] In this position, we waited for daylight to attack.[15]

The three brigades march through the woods was not easy and turned out to be chaotic, risking being surprised by the foot jäger and two battalions of Hesse and Hanover grenadiers that the Duke of Cumberland had placed in the woods south of Scheckenberg. Mercoyrol de Beaulieu's account adds more detail to the story:

> M. de Chevert [had ordered] that the two brigades under his command stand ready to march, that there should be as few horses as possible led to this march. Two hundred Volontaires, under the orders of M. de Rocqueval, *capitaine* of Picardie, had been moved forward at ten o'clock and came to take up position on the edge of the wood and the bottom of the heights occupied by the left of the enemy army, whose troops we had seen during the day were no more than a thousand or twelve hundred paces away.[16] At eleven o'clock at night, these two brigades in column, broken up by company, began to march and, the aim being to turn the left of the enemies, they came to pass along the wood which they occupied (this wood extended to their right by cultivated ground which was not

---

12   Charles-Joseph-Hyacinthe du Houx, Baron de Vioménil (1734-1827) was *colonel en second* of the *Volontaires de Dauphiné* in 1761, a *brigadier* in 1770, *maréchal de camp* in 1780, emigrated in 1791 and appointed *Maréchal de France* in 1816.
13   Alexis Magallon de La Morlière (1707-1799), was *colonel* of the Fusiliers de La Morlière in 1745, a *brigadier* from 1747, commander of the Volontaires de Flandre from their formation in 1749 which were made up of his Fusiliers, the Volontaires Bretons and the Arquebusiers de Grassin. He was promoted *maréchal de camp* in 1759, *lieutenant-général* in 1762. He was commanded the Armée du Rhin during the Revolution from 1792 to 1793.
14   François Henri Thiersaint, Baron de Bourgmary, was born in 1716. He was a *brigadier* from 1748 and made commander of the Volontaires de Flandre in 1749. The Volontaires de Flandres was split into two on 25 March 1757. Bourgmary took command of the second part which became the Volontaires du Hainault. He was wounded and taken prisoner at Minden, returning to France in December 1758 when he retired from service.
15   Valfons, *Souvenirs du marquis de Valfons*, pp.268-269.
16   Joseph-Salomon Fabre de Rocqueval was born in Florac in 1723. He volunteered for the Régiment de Picardie in 1741, became a *lieutenant* in 1742, *capitaine* in 1745. He became *lieutenant-colonel* of the Grenadiers Royaux de la Guyenne in 1771. He was *réformé* [put in reserve on half-pay] in 1775 and obtained the rank of *maréchal de camp* upon his retirement in 1791.

four hundred paces wide, then the woods resumed).[17] The path that the column was obliged to take skimmed the wood where the enemies were on its left; it was so narrow, so stony, so deep that for the most part it was hardly possible to walk two men abreast, which caused a continuous procession, although there were very few horses in this column, because all the officers who were able to march were on foot; but several of them had ordered their servants on horseback, who led them by hand, to follow the column; the other servants and their horses were therefore separated, which caused continual neighing. I affirm that these two brigades marched in the greatest disorder, it was impossible to do otherwise, with a noise of mess tins and cans and clash of weapons by the frequent falls that the soldiers made in this poor way. Silence was observed and I attribute it to the danger that everyone saw in this march, without forgetting to curse the neighing of the horses. If each officer had left his horses in the wood that we were leaving, the march would have been more secret, and I must say that the most part of those in the Picardie Brigade had taken this decision.

After having climbed one after the other in this disorder for half an hour, rather quickly, as every man imagined himself having his throat cut, the first battalion emerged onto a small plain of cultivated fields, holding it for those following who were to our right. As the companies came out of this defile and formed by company, the columns extended to the right, we came close to the wood at the end of this gap. The four battalions of the Régiment de Picardie held all the ground, roughly speaking, between the two woods; the enemy were in the one we had just passed which was on our left. This first formed brigade moved forward about sixty paces to make way for Navarre which formed the second line, and all the horses which belonged to these two brigades were placed in the slope of the gap, behind Navarre and, as this land was without the slightest resource to feed them, the neighing was continual.

Despite all the noise that had been made, we had not found any enemy on our route, having skirted round them under the branches of the wood which they occupied by the sunken path of which I have just spoken and there being no one of them at this edge of the woods. This was incredible negligence on their part (or so it seemed, and was an idea that we could not overcome) and led General Chevert to believe that they must be in full march to Hanover, as he had always thought they were. His persuasion in this regard was so constant that by putting the two brigades under his command in line, their front was facing the Hanover Road and their backs partly to the wood where the enemies were. The night was spent in this position; the soldiers were allowed to sit; tired of all the marching of the day before and the days before that, they soon fell asleep.

The eight guns from these two brigades climbed the mountain in turn, not without much noise, and the continual silence from the enemies increasingly confirmed that they must have left their position of the day before.[18]

The night was of benefit to the artillery. As well as positioning for the next day to fire on the Obensburg plateau battery, Vallière skilfully employed the

---

17 This was the gap above Voremberg which linked to the Hanover road by a pass through the village of Bisperode.
18 Vogüe & Sourd, *Campagnes de Mercoyrol de Beaulieu*, pp.128-131.

irregularities of the terrain, studied that afternoon, and had epaulements erected at two well-chosen points where he put 8-pounders to counter the two large enemy batteries erected behind and to the east of the village of Hastenbeck.

9

The Battle of Hastenbeck

Chevert and d'Armentières' attack on the day of the battle was sound; it would have been sufficient for a decisive victory if it had been supported by sixty squadrons of cavalry, useless no doubt for the attack on the heights, but necessary for descending to pursue the enemy and deciding the victory. The moral effect produced by the Duke of Brunswick with 1,200 men gave the Duke of Cumberland time to retire, and almost decided the fate of the battle. It proved the French officers' lack of experience; despite Chevert's presence.[1]

At dawn on 26 July, thick fog filled the plain and ravines. To reach the heights above the enemy battery, Chevert's troops still had an hour-and-a-half march through thick woods, in the midst of rocks and ravines to reach the plateau and in the hope of 'arranging a frontage of half a battalion at its smallest width'. These woods were precisely where enemy jäger and grenadiers were positioned. The troops would then have to descend on the left wing of the enemy by a steep path and a ravine which had not been previously scouted.[2]

The Duc de Randan was holding the extreme right between the villages of Voremberg and Bisperode on the road to Hanover, surveying the valley east of the Schekenberg, and 'was due to pass by the mountains up to Halle, turning at the one where the enemies were positioned to take them from behind but as the ground was not known and he was marching without a guide, he arrived on the morning of the battle alongside our army closer to us than to the enemies'.[3] As a result, the *Maréchal* sent his aide-de-camp Menil-Durand to order the advance of the Duc de Randan's d'Eu Brigade, comprising the regiment of that name and that of Engien, to reinforce Chevert's attacking division.

At daybreak, *Maréchal* d'Estrées assembled his other *lieutenant-généraux* for the last time to give them their orders.

As Chevert set off he received reinforcements from the Régiments d'Eu and Enghien, just beyond the village of Voremberg. The Comte de Lorges,

---

1 Napoleon, *Précis des guerres de Frédéric II, commentaires sur la guerre de Sept ans*, p.42.
2 Letter from an unknown officer in Duc de Luynes, *Memoires du Duc de Luynes*, Vol.XVI, p.131.
3 Chapotte, *Sous Louis le Bien-Aimé*, p.77.

who would have preferred to see command of this flanking force entrusted to his brother, the Duc de Randan, preceded d'Eu and Engien by an hour but listened little and very impatiently to Chevert explaining the terrain and the plan of attack. The size of the column had now increased from 12 to 16 battalions, in addition to the light troops. Mercoyrol de Beaulieu outlined their dispositions and movements:

> Shortly before daylight, M. de Bussy, who commanded 400 volunteers from the army, joined M. de Chevert, where he and his troops were placed on the left of the two infantry brigades. When M. de Bussy had positioned his troops here, with his own left supported by the woods, he took it into his head, as a man of war, to push 30 volunteers into the wood, with orders to scout ahead, since the disposition we held appeared to him unusual, except that one was not sure of the retreat of the enemy.
>
> Daylight was beginning to appear. The thirty volunteers in a small platoon had not walked a hundred paces in the woods, when we heard a few shots fired. As the greater part of the officers and soldiers had slept two or three hours and had awakened, the two brigades were soon standing at their arms, each having rested holding them covered to protect them from damp of the night, as each individual officer had recommended to his troops; the *capitaines* immediately made an inspection to check the priming was dry and to remedy those which were not through neglect.
>
> During this time, M. de Bussy broke the line he was holding [and instead] arranged his troops facing the wood, ordering fifty more men march into the trees, to support the first thirty he had sent there, with orders, as the general had prescribed to him, to be on the defensive and not to advance further into the wood, so that it would not be revealed that there was appearance of force so near and behind the enemy left; this was executed with intelligence, and the two brigades remained in the position they held during the night, as the lack of guard of the edge of the wood confirmed to everyone that the enemy had withdrawn. The first enemy discovered in the wood had a continual small skirmish with the thirty men of M. de Bussy but as the soldiers on both sides took a good big trees to take cover and tried to shoot with advantage, they hardly fired one or two musket shots per minute and so the noise that the enemies necessarily had to hear did not give them any alarm by its mediocrity, especially as it was fixed in the same place.
>
> As the day grew brighter, M. de Chevert walked to the gap behind us; he saw part of the French army which formed his line and also saw the right of the enemy army in the same position it had held the day before, as well as the centre and the left, which he had not been able to see, because of the mountain and the woods we were next to; he judged that everyone should remain in the same order as the day before and gaining this knowledge saw that the knives were out and there would be a battle. He had orders from *Maréchal* d'Estrées for this eventuality, as well as if it was the case that the enemy had withdrawn. Everything had been planned in the council of war held the day before in the presence of the Duc d'Orléans, first prince of the blood.
>
> Returning from his observations, as the sun then hit the horizon, he [Chevert] ordered the Picardie and Navarre brigades to form a column by battalion to the front, the first [battalion] of Picardie holding [the head], the others in succession

and afterwards, the four Navarre [battalions]. The two other infantry brigades were yet to arrive, first that of the Vieille Marine,[4] which only reached us at seven o'clock; they were under the orders of M. de Maupeou, who informed us of the imminent arrival of d'Eu and Enghien led by M. de Randan. These two brigades had marched under the orders of the latter general [Randan] to cover the right of the army after it had left Halle and had had to march in echelons as they could not arrive together, which delayed the start of M. Chevert's attack, which rightly gave him great annoyance and impatience, the enemy being able to help themselves to an increase of troops and obstacles on their left.

The La Marine Brigade took the same formation as Picardie and Navarre by forming column by battalion to the front. D'Eu had not yet appeared, giving M. de Chevert plenty of time to [order] the *colonels* and *lieutenant-colonels* to meet him; they arrived and M. de Chevert said: "What we do today depends on the continued glory of the King's arms, with the oldest and most senior phalanxes of the State at your command. You can see our position and that we are, by the march executed during the night, on the left flank and even behind this wing of the enemy. Our attack must be as swift as lightning; we must not fire muskets at them, but, keep moving forward through the wood before us, reach the enemy and drive him out with bayonets. I therefore ask for your word, Gentlemen, that you will lead your troops in this way; let each of you go to your regiment to assemble the officers there to make your own promise, for each *capitaine* to pass on this message to his company. I warn you further that the beginning of our attack will decide the march and the attacks of the army." These points agreed upon, each *colonel* went to his regiment to assemble his officers and repeated what Général Chevert had demanded of them, asking them to make the same promise. All agreed, the officers were at their posts. At this point d'Eu Brigade emerged from a small grove a quarter of a league from us. M. de Chevert ordered nine companies of grenadiers, three from each of the first three brigades under the orders of M. le Comte du Châtelet,[5] which lined up at the head of the column, in front of the first Picardie battalion, and formed the first echelon of the column formed from these four brigades.[6] The cannon of each brigade had to march in the woods, on the flank, and could only be accomplished by meandering and by the skill of the drivers. M. de Bussy, with the 400 men at his command, was in front of everyone.[7]

---

4 Translator's note: Mercoyrol refers to La Marine here as *Vieille* [Old] Marine as it was one of the most senior regiments of the army, established in 1635, thus distinguishing it from the more recently-raised Régiment Royal Marine.

5 Louis-Marie-Florent de Lomont d'Haraucourt (1727-1793), Comte du Châtelet, was the son of the Madame de Breteuil, Marquise du Châtelet, a woman of letters and lover of Voltaire. Châtelet was *colonel* of the Régiment de Navarre. He was promoted to *brigadier* on 9 August 1757, *colonel* of the Régiment du Roi in 1767, *maréchal de camp* in 1761, ambassador to England in 1768, Duc du Châtelet in 1770, *lieutenant-général* in 1780 and *commandant* of the Gardes Françaises in 1788. He was guillotined on the 13 December 1793.

6 There were actually, 12 companies of grenadiers, i.e. three companies from each of the four brigades according to the plan of attack made by the Marquis de Valfons in his archives (see Appendix VI). There were three companies of grenadiers out of four from each of the Régiments de Picardie, La Marine and Navarre, both companies of the Régiment d'Eu and one of the two from Enghien (there was one companies of grenadiers per battalion).

7 Vogüe & Sourd, *Campagnes de Mercoyrol de Beaulieu*, pp.131-135.

HASTENBECK 1757

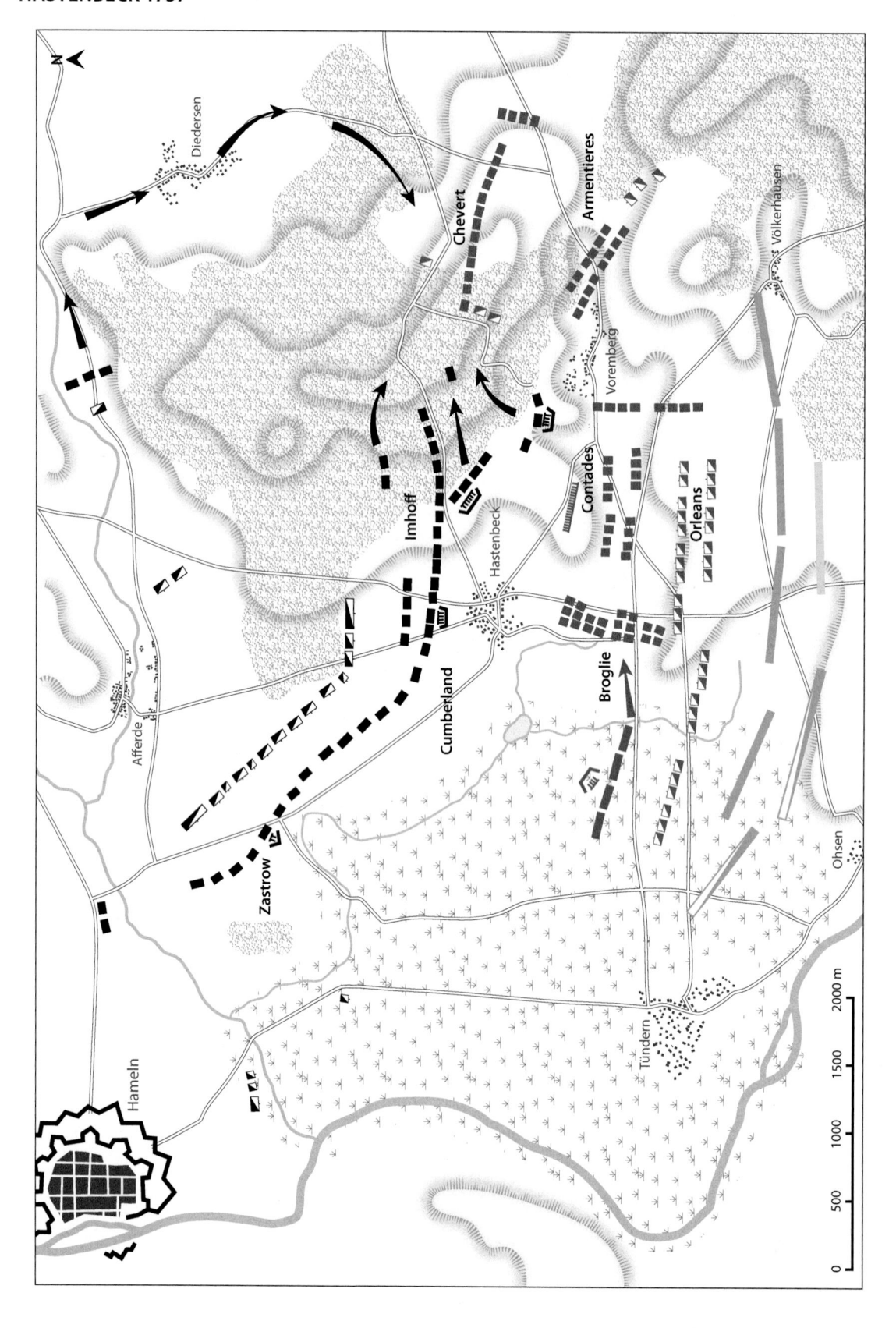

Chevert set the column into motion in unison. The Volontaires de Flandres and Hainaut served as scouts for the grenadier companies entrusted to the Comte du Châtelet, *colonel* of Navarre, and to *lieutenant-colonel* de Gascoing, of Picardie, which were followed by the battalions de Picardie, La Marine, d'Eu and Enghien, dragging their guns with them; the Régiment de Navarre followed as rear guard.[8]

The Hanoverian batteries opened fire at 5.30 a.m. The French batteries responded sporadically, waiting for the first cannon shot from Chevert's column, on the right, as the signal for the general attack, expected around 8.00 a.m. The Hanoverian artillery fire was quickly directed against the French batteries, in particular those of the Duc de Broglie's reserve, which was advanced on the plain on the French left:

> As soon as the very thick fog dissipated around seven o'clock, the battery of eight 8pdrs commanded by M. du Teil who was directly on my left began to fire, it was fiercely attacked by a battery of eight or nine 12pdrs, which the enemy sited on the plain, to the left of us from the village of Hastenbeck, and by another battery on the enemy left near the wood which targeted ours *en rouage*.[9]

Chevert's attack column was moving along the edge of the woods by battalion, the first Picardie battalion in the lead. The battalions split into *pelotons* cross the thickets and came to face the enemy left wing, in several columns. The enemy positions in the woods were expected to be fortified and protected by multiple abatis but few were found to exist and they were not much of an obstacle. Nothing seemed to have been prepared to make the woods and thickets impenetrable. Mercoyrol de Beaulieu picks up the story again:

> The order was given; all shook themselves and began to move. Two hundred paces into the woods a fusillade began between the [enemy] troops there and those under the orders of M. de Bussy, who was killed. This formidable column continued to march. The 400 men of the late M. de Bussy, one half supporting the right and the other on the left, continued to fire while marching forward and, at the head of the column which kept its promise to march without firing, the first echelon of the troops found there joined a second which supported it and they rallied there so the fire became more considerable. At this point it must be said that the ground was steadily rising very gradually, which gave the enemies the opportunity for a great deal of fire, but it did little harm as the wood partially protected us. The column still kept to its word here and, continuing its march, proceeding with a decided step, and a very confident countenance. At four paces the enemies made an about face and withdrew. The column had to keep driving and certainly would have done so having already marched together for two

---

[8] In his report of 28 July to the Minister, Chevert wrote that he had left Navarre to the rear, which justified depriving it of their *colonel* to command the grenadiers in the column. Waddington, *La guerre de sept ans*, p.430.

[9] Duc de Broglie to the Minister, in Duteil, *Une famille militaire au XVIIIe siècle*, p.57. Translator's note: *En rouage* [cog] refers to a military term to refer to counter-battery fire where the gunners attempt to destroy the enemy guns. Perhaps *rouage* was used to refer to smashing the guns down to their constituent parts.

hundred paces, but the grenadiers who took the lead unfortunately stopped and began some very lively musketry. As the fire of the enemies fell over the centre, these grenadiers, to avoid the danger, gradually moved, some to the right, others to the left, and came upon about four *pelotons* of the first battalion in the centre, where I was ordering my own. M. de Bréhant, who was to the right of his first battalion, came to the centre and said to me: "Why then this fusillade?" and pointing to those firing, "I am going to them," he said to me, "to tell the officers, if possible, to make them march forward." I could see that many, who were kneeling and gave the impression that they could not hear anything, would press to the right and left, as de Bussy's volunteers had done, and that the uncovered column would move forward, and our centre would get bogged down in this place which was a dangerous thing for order would be broken and that, if we came across a strong force, it could become dangerous. At this moment our four cannons, which were on the right, fired. The four guns of Navarre joined them and made a terrible uproar, which echoed and multiplied the noise. The enemy were fighting from behind some trees they had cut down on the right; About forty made a sortie, charging our artillery, seized two horses near us, no doubt with the intention of taking them away, and captured le chevalier Le Prêtre, aged seventeen.[10] However a company of grenadiers from the Régiment de Picardie fell on these brave men and, with bayonets, soon made them vanish; most of those who performed this valiant act were killed.[11]

It was 8:30 a.m. The volunteers had chased away the enemy outposts who, firing before withdrawing, had triggered the response of the French grenadiers.

Several other accounts mention Bussy's death. An unknown officer wrote that 'M. de Bussy had already been wounded by three musket shots; he found himself between two lots of fire he was killed by the fourth musket shot along with almost all of his volunteers, from whom only two officers and twenty men returned.'[12] The Marquis de Valfons went into rather more detail:

> They came to tell Chevert that Bussy had been killed; hiding his fears from those around him, he said to me: "He was our only guide, that cannot be. Valfons, go get him!" I had not gone a hundred paces into the woods when I found him on foot, it was true that his horse had been shot in the mouth, reared up and knocked him over, but he was not injured; I led him to M. de Chevert who, pretending to have some orders to give him, was very happy to show him to our troops; he then sent him back to his post, where a few moments later he was killed by eight musket shots at the first discharge …
>
> The death of de Bussy put us in terrible trouble which we had to hide. He was our guide and the only one who knew the terrain because the hussar sent out the

---

10   François-Charles Le Prestre de Jaucourt, (1740-1814), Baron de Théméricourt was *enseigne* in the Régiment de Picardie in 1756, became *lieutenant* on 24 February 1757, *aide-major* in 1761, *capitaine* in 1762, *major* of Picardie in 1778, *lieutenant-colonel* of the Régiment de Blaisois in 1784 then of the Régiment de Provence. He was *colonel* of the 28e Infanterie de Ligne (formerly Maine) from 1791 to 1793.
11   Vogüe & Sourd, *Campagnes de Mercoyrol de Beaulieu*, pp.135-137.
12   Unidentified letter in Duc de Luynes, *Memoires du Duc de Luynes*, Vol.XVI, p.131.

day before had already been killed. What gave me the most confidence was the firmness of the infantry, which, despite the liveliness of the fire, boldly advanced forward to support the grenadiers.[13]

Chevert's column had advanced towards the top of the mountain. When his regimental pieces began firing on the enemy, they had given the signal for the French attack. Vallière's artillery began their own fire with accuracy and liveliness, gradually gaining superiority over the enemy artillery.

The Marquis d'Armentières advanced in front of the easternmost Hanoverian battery, which was already raining fire. On the far right, the attack on the plateau at the top of Obensburg was beginning in earnest for Chevert's column. Sensing the danger to his left, the Duke of Cumberland had sent his foot jäger into the woods around 7:00 a.m., sent all the grenadiers in his reserve to reinforce then, and advanced five more infantry battalions of the second line to his right.[14]

Seconding Chevert, as *major-génénal* or chief of staff, was the Marquis de Valfons. He recounted the difficulties encountered going forward:

> We had hardly entered the woods when the enemies appeared, numbering two thousand Hessians supported by eight Hanoverian battalions, their right against sheer rock more than forty feet high; this cut through the wood, secured their right and rear. In front of them were large standing oaks, and between the voids other felled oaks formed formidable abattis; a thicket that could not be penetrated completed their terrain. The ground we could occupy was a clearing, where we were visible to our toes ... The skill of Chevert and his experience had foreseen and prepared for such a salutary movement, he had told me by putting the infantry in column, to leave a gap between each battalion so at the first discharge all could go forward with ease as the soldiers believed they were gaining ground as the enemy was fleeing; this idea made him redouble their ardour; but in fact it was only the space that we filled by moving into the gaps. All marched through wooded and unknown terrain, where the desire to conquer made them push deeper; we had to throw ourselves on the right; but every time we left the thicket, we fell back into the light woods, where the enemy crushed us. I dismounted and gave my cuirass to two grenadiers of d'Eu who were killed.[15]

After the grenadier engagement which cleared the way the march, Chevert's corps set out forward again in column by battalion which divided its frontage into *pelotons* to penetrate the thickets. The Régiment de Picardie was still in the lead, led by its colonel:

---

13 Valfons, *Souvenirs du marquis de Valfons*, pp.270-272.
14 There were two grenadier battalions, from Hesse (1) and Hanover (1), and the foot jäger protecting the Graf von Schulenburg's eastern battery, made up of two 12-pounders, two 6-pounders and two howitzers. They were reinforced in the woods by five battalions of grenadiers which until then had been held in reserve, from Brunswick (2), Hesse (1) and Hanover (2); plus, on the edge, at the foot of the western slope of the mountain, five infantry battalions from Brunswick (3) drawn from the second line and Hanover (2) from the right wing.
15 Valfons, *Souvenirs du marquis de Valfons*, pp.271-273.

> M. de Bréhant ... returned to the centre of the battalion and loudly said to me: "We are going to march forward." "Quickly," I said to the three *pelotons* which made up the left of the *battalion*, "If the grenadiers in front of you do not march, pass in front of them, without breaking." M. de Bréhant said the same to the two *pelotons* on the right, whose front was still covered by the grenadiers and, moving ten or twelve paces forward, took his sword in hand facing this first battalion, to order them forward; he was shot in the thigh, which was warded off by a gold seal in his trouser pocket, and he fell suddenly on his rump. My attachment and esteem for this *colonel* made me run to him, believing him to be seriously injured. He had fallen twenty paces from the enemies. My enthusiasm mingled with the feelings I had for him; I placed myself between him and the enemy ... twenty balls came ploughing through the grass beside us ... he saw the danger and, supporting himself with a tree branch, I put my two arms under his, holding him from behind. While standing, he moved both legs to see if there is any fracture; he found them both free from this accident; I grabbed him under the arm and help him to return to the *battalion*, when we arrived, I made the lines of my company squeeze together, to allow him pass behind and gave him a soldier from my company to lend him his arm ... The next moment we learned that M. de Gascoing, our *lieutenant-colonel*, seconded to the grenadiers under M. le Comte du Châtelet ... had just been killed. At the same instant the same M. du Châtelet, supported under each arm by two officers of the Régiment de Navarre, came towards us, his thigh and boot covered with blood, having a shot in the groin. Approaching us, he said to these officers in a very distinct voice, "You must know how to give your blood and your life for the service of your prince." I opened the lines of my company and they passed behind ... M. de Chevert, on horseback, arrived opposite my *peloton*. Seeing him, the enemy redoubled their fire to try to bring him down; I saw the general without a cuirass (he only had the *collet* around his collar), and his red sash over his coat ... It occurred to me: If our general was unfortunately killed or seriously injured here, who would give us his orders? (We didn't have a single *maréchal de camp* for our two brigades) ... addressing M. de Chevert, I said, "Général, this is the road by which MM. de Bréhant and du Châtelet passed just now; since you want to talk to them, you cannot fail to find them." I pointed the way. He stared at me from head to toe and walked by. I affected to straighten myself up as much as possible, in order to show him that my fear was only for him but in truth I felt it too.[16]

The losses were severe among the grenadiers who, after the light troops, suffered the most fire from the enemy positions.

> Of the eleven *capitaines* of the grenadiers, four were killed in the action, as well as d'Ablancourt, of the Régiment de Navarre, de Camps of La Marine and d'Ortan, of d'Eu. The wounded were the Chevalier d'Urre,[17] [Dallenne],[18] from Picardie;

---

16 Vogüe & Sourd, *Campagnes de Mercoyrol de* Beaulieu, pp.137-140.
17 Laurent, Chevalier d'Urre, born in 1716, entered the Régiment de Picardie as *lieutenant en second* in 1733. He became a *lieutenant* in 1734, *capitaine* in 1740, then *capitaine de grenadiers* from 24 March 1757. He would command the battalion in 1759 and left with its reduction in 1763.
18 Procope Le Rique Dallenne, born in 1711, entered the Régiment de Picardie as *lieutenant en second* in 1734 He became a *lieutenant* the same year. He was promoted to *capitaine* in 1742,

Coupenne, from Navarre; [Darnans],[19] [de] Vignacourt, of La Marine; Gressian of the régiment d'Eu; Lammerville,[20] alone, of the Régiment d'Enghien, although full of valour, was not touched.[21]

A company of Picardie grenadiers under the orders of *Capitaine* Dallenne, having lost their way in the thickets, had turned north and found themselves facing a strong enemy party. Fearing that he would be cut off if he tried to re-join the column, Dallenne stood firm in the face of the enemy persuading them that he was supported. By doing this he had covered the right flank of the column, but the company was crushed, Dallene was shot in the shoulder and his *lieutenant* and his *sous-lieutenant* put out of action, but his *sergent* continued the company's fire until the column took the Obensburg and the enemy withdrawn. Chevert's column, stopped in the forest by the musketry for a time, faced an opening, as they marched, firing in files by *peloton* by the first Picardie battalion which led the column. Again, Mercoyrol de Beaulieu picks up the story:

> We stayed in position for another quarter of an hour. The enemy who, by continual fire, had greatly reduced the frontage of the grenadier companies in front of us, seeing that the head of our column persevered in holding their fire, noticed that by making the good adjustment of lowering their aim, they had previously fired horizontally straight ahead which did not cause us much injury, and as they were only thirty-five or forty paces away, they immediately brought down fifty or sixty men of the battalion. M. Gelb, a brave *aide-major*, arrived where I was, observed that after two minutes the faces of the soldiers, until then ruddy, had become visibly white.[22] Seeing no senior officer, I said to Gelb, "Listen, I say we open fire. The enemies shoot us, let's give them the same goods. Tell the Denocq *peloton*, which still had grenadiers in front of them, and the Paluette *peloton*, on its right, not to fire.[23] I will warn the Chevalier de Monteil to prevent his people firing for the same reason."[24] And so, running to the front of the battalion, I warned the

---

    he became *capitaine de grenadiers* and commanded a battalion in 1761 and left active service in 1762.

19 Emmanuel Dominique Dussaix, Comte de Darnans, was born in 1713. He was *lieutenant* in the Régiment de La Marine in 1730, *capitaine* in 1733, *capitaine de grenadiers* in 1751, commanded a battalion in 1758 and left active service in 1765.

20 François Auson de Lammerville, was born in 1705. He was a *lieutenant* in Enghien in 1728, *aide-major* in 1731, *capitaine* in 1734, he moved company in 1740 and became *capitaine de grenadiers* from 1748. He commanded a battalion in 1758, was *colonel* of the regiment in 1760, *brigadier* in 1761 and *maréchal de camp* in 1762.

21 Valfons, *Souvenirs du marquis de Valfons*, pp.271-272. See the table of French losses in Appendix VII.

22 Jean-Joseph Gelb was *lieutenant* of the Régiment de Picardie in 1743, *capitaine* in 1746, *aide-major* in 1747, *major de la place* of Göttingen in 1761 where he was killed in a sortie under the orders of the Vicomte de Belzunce.

23 Jacques Framery Denocq *capitaine* of the Régiment de Picardie, retired in 1765. Jean-Baptiste de la Paluette de Coatquin was born in 1718. He became a *sous-lieutenant* of the Régiment de Picardie in 1735, *enseigne* in 1736, *lieutenant* in 1738, *capitaine* in 1743, a *capitaine de grenadiers* in 1761, *breveté major* in 1765 and retired in 1766.

24 Anne-Antoine de Monteil (1722-1786) was a *lieutenant* in 1741, *capitaine* in the Régiment de Picardie in 1743, and became *lieutenant du Roi* at Narbonne in 1760.

Chevalier de Monteil and the others that we were going to start *peloton* fire just as the exercise. Returning to my troops, I give the usual command to my *peloton* and the fire followed from the indicated wings, after which I began again. Four discharges from the five *pelotons* were able to drive the enemies ahead of us away and, instead of beginning a fifth volley, I listened: Not a shot. I looked through the leaves and branches of the felled trees opposite, I no longer saw the enemy where they were before. I said to my *peloton*, which was prepared to continue fire, "Shoulder your arms and, if they start again, we will answer them."

At this moment, M. de Bréhant, whose wound was a contusion, arrived. I give him an account of the fire that he had just heard and that, if he wished to order a march forward, I was sure that the enemies would have made the same manoeuvre as Bussy's volunteers and the nine compagnies of grenadiers and were thrown to the left and right to avoid the fire which was heating them up; he gave the command in a loud voice: "*En avant, marche!*" which the battalion briskly carried out. We seized the ground held by the enemy and found them, as I had judged, returning to their posts which our fire had made them abandon; then a cry of: "Kill, kill!" was the signal for their flight. We pushed them up to the top of the mountain where they are knocked back over on the peak; the bayonet had been used to hunt and destroy them, and then shooting accompanied their descent over the other side. On the height, where all the French army could see us if they had looked there, M. de Chevert ordered that the colours of the first *battalion* be flown, which was carried out; In addition, M. de Chevert had the four pieces of cannon of the Picardie Brigade manhandled there, which fired several shots against the rear and flank of the enemy army.

We had only six *pelotons* of the 1st battalion [of Picardie] and three compagnies of grenadiers from La Marine on top of the mountain … three battalions of Picardie followed two *pelotons* of the first battalion, which followed the grenadiers, and Navarre followed these Picardie battalions. La Marine moved more to the left and found itself on the left of Navarre and, as a battalion of the La Marine was in front of it and on its right, the thick copses obscured its view; they thought that they were enemies and as a result the battalion unleashed all its fire on Navarre who, being shot from behind, did not know what to think, which created disorder in this regiment and even more astonishment, but because the thicket that separated them was very thick and stopped almost all the balls it did not cause a lot of trouble. As this discharge had happened without orders, the officers of this corps prevented any more fire, and the Navarre battalion which received this discharge descended halfway down the mountain, where it joined the three other battalions.[25]

Below the Scheckenberg, the Marquis d'Armentières' corps, volunteer grenadiers with *Capitaine* de Rocqueval at the head as the day before, made a frontal attack on the easternmost Hanoverian battery, near the village of Voremberg. The position had already been damaged by French artillery fire. The Graf von Schulenburg who commanded the position was at the point of being pushed north by the dual attacks of Chevert's column and the grenadiers

---

25 Vogüé & Sourd, *Campagnes de Mercoyrol de Beaulieu*, pp. 140-143.

of the Marquis d'Armentières' corps. Schulenburg was forced to retreat but managed to pull his guns back, with only one dismantled piece falling into French hands. However, after its initial success the Marquis d'Armentières' corps got lost as it continued its advance. It was a predictable error in unscouted rugged terrain combined with a desire to close with Chevert who was attacking on the other flank, which made d'Armentiéres deviate to the right and into the woods where he was no longer visible by the rest of the army. As Valfons wrote:

> The three columns of the left positioned on the side of the mountain, to support our attack with theirs, made no movement, except the one closest to us, commanded by M. d'Armentières and composed of the Régiments de Belzunce and Alsace who made a mistake, instead of walking parallel to us, turned to the right and arrived behind us.[26]

The Marquis d'Armentières was warned of this error and moved his column obliquely to his left and continued his attack.

Finally, the rest of the army advanced under the orders of *Maréchal* d'Estrées, who remained on the Bückeberg, above Hagenohsen which overlooked the entire plain, facing the village of Hastenbeck. His first line was composed entirely of infantry and his second of cavalry.

The Comte de Maillebois, having noticed the danger to the line caused by d'Armentières movements, proposed to *Maréchal* d'Estrées that the gap created in the first line should be filled with the four battalions of the Champagne Brigade and the four others of the Swiss brigade, the Régiments de Reding and Salis. Until then these had been in the centre reserve. D'Estrées agreed to the proposal.

The artillery in front of the infantry progressed from ravine to ravine, taking advantage of the locations noted the day before by Vallière, and continued to strike down the enemy. Vallière never left his batteries. The French cannonballs fell on the redoubts and the enemy's first line, then ricocheted into the squadrons placed in the second line. Reaching a high point opposite Hastenbeck, the French artillery continued its sharp and well-aimed fire which slashed through the battalions in front of it and shook up the Hessian cavalry, which was out of range beyond the village. The Chevalier de Tourny, *capitaine* in the Regiment d'Aquitaine Cavalerie, described the scene to his father:

> One of our [batteries], the main one, advanced on the hedgerows of Hastenbeck and, although it was caught between two enemy batteries which had a greater number of guns and of larger calibres, it fired with so much order, vivacity and success that it repeatedly set fire to the powder of one of the opposing batteries, dismantled and silenced it: M. du Teil, who commanded this battery, deserves much honour; he placed ricochets so well that his cannon balls flew at the battery, then passed through the battalions and were lost in the cavalry. Our artillery

---

26 Valfons, *Souvenirs du marquis de Valfons*, p.273.

cannot be praised enough, it did a lot of damage to the enemies and, by drawing all their fire to it, saved a lot of infantry and cavalry for the King.[27]

After raising the colours of the first Picardie battalion, which held the summit with three grenadier companies from La Marine, Chevert had the four regimental light guns open fire to their rear, on the enemy's centre, which faced south-west, and their left wing, which faced south-east, who were now attacked from both sides. This combined attack was completed with a final assault by the Régiment de Navarre, led by the Marquis de Valfons, who decisively drove the enemy from the entire ridge line, which he then held tenaciously:

> The pushed enemies retreated to a second height, with a ravine in front of them. I moved a little to our right with Chevert, at the head of the Régiment de Navarre … "The Régiment de Navarre awaits your orders to overthrow them all." A general officer whom I am not willing to name represented that he was losing Navarre, that the enemies were on them. "Even better, Monsieur," I told them eagerly, "let M. d'Estrées turn them across the plain, they will be prisoners." And immediately, by the order of M. de Chevert, I formed Navarre in several columns and the attack recommenced, this brave regiment crossed the ravine gaining the height, and with fixed bayonets, they fell upon and dispersed the enemies. At the top of the plateau I had an admirable view, the two armies firing at each other. Our fire, much brighter, imposed so strong on the opposing line of infantry, that it was wavering and in great disorder.[28]

The Marquis d'Armentières' division had chased the enemy beyond the easternmost battery and reached the redoubt where the second battery was positioned. All morning it had been subjected to the fire of 10 French 4-pounders which had gained the upper hand according to a Hanoverian officer: 'It was not like cannon shots, but a fire approaching that of a battalion firing by division … the boldest blow that I saw, was to pull, almost at the gallop, six 6pdrs onto the plain, in the open, and fire against our cannon and troops, in the teeth of a battery of ten 12-pounders'.[29] The Comte de Laval-Montmorency was shot dead in the left eye while carrying an order.[30] The Vicomte de Belzunce, stood in front of his regiment with the grenadiers, was wounded: seeing 'three men who were aiming at him; he ordered two grenadiers to shoot at them; these two grenadiers were killed, each with a musket shot, and he received a shot in his cane which, after having broken it, pierced his arm. Fortunately, his injury was not dangerous'.[31]

---

27 Tourny to his father in Duteil, *Une famille militaire au XVIIIe siècle*, p.469.
28 Valfons, *Souvenirs du marquis de Valfons*, pp.273-274.
29 Lucien Perey, *Un petit-neveu de Mazarin, Louis-Mazarini duc de Nivernais* (Paris: Calman Lévy, 1899), pp.433-434.
30 Joseph Pierre Comte de Laval-Montmorency (1729-1757) was *colonel* of the Régiment de Guyenne and employed on the staff as aide to the *maréchal-général des logis*.
31 Armand de Belzunce (1722-1763) was *colonel* of the regiment that took his name from 1749. He became *brigadier* in 1760, *maréchal de camp* in 1761 and, in command of the troops

The Marquis d'Anlézy, commanding the brigades of Champagne and Reding, was in the front line, between the Marquis de Contades in the centre and the Marquis d'Armentières on the right. D'Anlézy received the order to assault and hold the redoubt. The Régiment de Champagne took the lead, forming into column and with its grenadier companies in the vanguard. The four battalions of the two Swiss Régiments de Reding and Salis, advanced together in parallel to the right, along the flank, covered by the dismounted dragoons to the rear that the Marquis d'Armentières had left behind.

Around 11:00 a.m., the Régiment de Champagne raised it colours high and proudly advanced, through rough terrain between two ravines 'about twenty feet deep by twelve wide'.[32] Each time the head of the column reached the top of an escarpment which gave a view of the enemy, the regimental guns, transported by hand, were assembled in battery and opened fire allowing the men a few moments rest before resuming their gruelling march. However, the Régiment de Champagne, advancing faster than the Swiss column in the woods, soon found itself within range of three enemy battalions on its flank. One of these battalions was not spotted and opened fire. Taken by surprise, the soldiers of Champagne broke ranks and the battalions turned back to the ravine that they had just come from. *Pelotons* in front and to the right began a disorderly shootout with an enemy they could not see. A few interminable minutes passed, reckoned the Comte de Gisors, *colonel* of the regiment, before the officers were able to stop the fire. The woods were searched, but the enemy had withdrawn when the two Swiss and three regiments of dismounted dragoons arrived.

The Champagne battalions reformed in the ravine and left cover move forward again and reached the great redoubt. The grenadiers attacked. The Hanoverian artillery gave a single discharge before fleeing. The French grenadiers threw themselves into the ditch, scaled the parapet and hoisted themselves into the embrasures gaining the upper hand over their Hanoverian and Hessian counterparts and took control of the battery and its guns.

Now the young Erbprinz of Brunswick emerged from the weak second line behind the village of Hastenbeck, at the head of two battalions of his own Leib-Regiment and a third Hanoverian battalion.[33] Outnumbered, shot at point-blank range and assaulted with bayonets, the Champagne grenadiers were forced to withdraw. They reformed in a ravine to return to the assault, this time attempting to bypass the redoubt and enter through the gorge. At the same time, led by their *colonel*, the battalions of the Régiment de Champagne launched their attack, supported by the Régiment d'Alsace from the Marquis d'Armentières' division. The fusiliers crossed the ditch and the parapet to drive out the enemy for good, taking the eight 12-pounders and two howitzers which remained in the battery.

---

sent to America, left France in 1762 disembarking in Saint-Domingue. He became *lieutenant-général* and *gouverneur général* of the island where he died the following year.
32 'Hanoverian Journal', cited in Rousset, *Le comte de Gisors*, p.224.
33 Charles-Guillaume-Ferdinand de Brunswick-Wolfenbüttel (1735-1806), Duke of Brunswick-Lünebourg and Prince of Wolfenbüttel, known by the title of Erbprinz (crown prince) received his baptism of fire Hastenbeck which earned his great reputation. He was fatally wounded at Auerstedt on 14 October, 1806.

Maréchal d'Estrées moved to the redoubt to direct the battle which was now being fought on the heights of Hastenbeck village. The entire centre and left of the French army were now positioned in front of Hastenbeck. Between the village and the redoubt, the passage was barely 700 metres wide. Hastenbeck had been set ablaze when Cumberland's forces retreated earlier in the day. To allow his troops to emerge on this narrow frontage, d'Estrées formed three columns. The first was commanded by the Marquis de Contades with ten battalions, the Régiment du Roi at their head. The second column was made up of six *battalions* of the Grenadiers de France and the Grenadiers Royaux de Solar, under the orders of the Comte de Guerchy, and the third, commanded by the Duc de Broglie was eight battalions from his reserve, which marched between the first two columns. These three columns marched through this narrow space together. The light artillery of the Hessian regiments tried to stop them by firing grapeshot, but it was in vain and they were quickly driven away by French artillery fire.

At the same time, Chevert was preparing to descend from Obensburg to emerge onto the plain and flank the enemy. Leaving the d'Eu Brigade to guard the plateau and ridges, he formed his column with Picardie at the head followed by Navarre and then the La Marine Brigade. He took the regimental artillery trailing the *piquets* so as not to inconvenience them but use them to crush the enemy when taken from the flank:

> M. de Chevert said to M. de Randan, *lieutenant-général*, who had arrived with the d'Eu Brigade. "Take your post, Sir, on the summit of the height that I am leaving and place the brigade at your command as you deem appropriate." M. de Randan took his guns under his direct command on the plateau and took an additional four from La Marine at the suggestion of the general as the officer who commanded them was young and dared not refuse.[34]

The Duke of Cumberland was now threatened to be completely flanked on his left – his batteries there had been taken and his centre shaken by the artillery and frontal attack of the three columns – and so he began his withdrawal in very good order, bringing his right below Hameln and his left retreating in a northerly direction, along the Scheckenberg mountain to the village of Afferde. The Chevalier de Tournay wrote:

> Our infantry on the plain marched into the village of Hastenbeck and captured it along with a ten-gun battery of 13-pounders [sic]. The fire ceased at noon, the enemy infantry retreated through the woods back to their cavalry, and then fell back under Hameln's cannon.[35]

It was 11:30 a.m. and everything pointed to a decisive victory for the French, whose lead columns had passed Hastenbeck and reached the sunken lane beyond the village. The cavalry followed, impatient to charge the enemy squadrons that had been in line in front of them since morning behind

---

34 Vogüé & Sourd, *Campagnes de Mercoyrol de Beaulieu*, p.146.
35 Tournyto his father in Duteil, *Une famille militaire au XVIIIe siècle*, p.469.

the batteries, on the Sintelberg plateau to the west and the foothills of Schmiedebrink to the east.

The Duke of Cumberland had placed six squadrons and three Hanoverian battalions to the rear extreme left of his line, at the defile of Schecken separating the northern slope of the Scheckenberg from the neighbouring heights and into which the Bisperode valley began. Two of the four squadrons of the Breidenbach Dragoon Regiment, and three battalions of the Sporcken, Zandré and Hardenberg Regiments were placed at the foot of the northern slope of the Scheckenberg, above the village of Diedersen, under the orders of *Oberst* von Breidenbach;[36] four squadrons of the Schlütter and Dachenhausen cavalry regiments under *Oberst* von Dachenhausen were in support at Afferde, one kilometre behind, to the west.[37]

A little after 10:00 a.m., having seen the French emerge on the peaks of Scheckenberg, the Duke of Cumberland ordered *Oberst* von Breidenbach to advance. He marched on Diedersen, where he found no one, then bypassed the massif to the east and the Bisperode valley. Arriving southeast of Scheckenberg, the infantry ascended the Obensburg marching to the sound of musketry as the six squadrons advanced to the pass above Voremberg.

Ascending from the east was as difficult and long as it had been for Chevert's column. When the three battalions reached the top, their grenadier comrades from Hanover, Hesse and Brunswick had already fully withdrawn. The column of Picardie, Navarre, and La Marine began their descent from the western slope to attack from the flank. *Oberst* von Breidenbach took by surprise the d'Eu Brigade who was losing its discipline, with soldiers coming out to seek shade or water who found themselves being picked off; the Régiment de Enghien had become separated from d'Eu and was forced to descend the ravine. Panic-stricken, the brigade was put into disorder. Again, Mercoyrol de Beaulieu adds more details:

> No sooner was M. de Randan established [on the Obensburg plateau] when the chiefs of the two regiments he commanded came to ask his permission to fetch water from a small stream they had passed very close to where we had been in contact the night before. M. de Randan allowed four or five soldiers per company at a time, who hastened to take canteens and, to hasten them, took off their *gibernes* [ammunition boxes] and *habits* [coats]. M. de Randan and the officers with him, who saw the enemy army withdrawing from their peak, did not notice that almost all the soldiers of this brigade had laid down their *gibernes* and *habits*; they certainly were not expecting what befell them. In this state they sat down and impatiently awaited the return of those who had been to fetch water.
>
> The Chevalier de Grammont, of the Régiment d'Enghien, a very alert young man, had advanced into the middle of the wood, saw a column of [soldiers]

---

36 Maximillian Johann Christian von Breidenbach died a *Generalmajor* in 1759.
37 Schlütter's colonel, Johann Conrad von Schlütter (1699-1757) was a month earlier at Pyrmont, between Detmold and Bodenwerder on 23 June. Carl Gustav von Dachenhausen was pensioned as a *Generalmajor* in 1759. He was the brother of Johann Heinrich von Dachenhausen, colonel of the regiment of dragoons that bore his name. He and his regiment were placed on the right flank at Hastenbeck, protecting the bridge over the Hamel, and he died a *Generalmajor* in 1758.

dressed in red approaching him;[38] the caps on their head in no way resembled those of the Swiss in the service of France;[39] he ran to carry the alarm to his brigade, shouting, "To arms; the enemy!" and, taking the first four soldiers he found, he marched up to the column, crying: "Who goes there?" The column continued its march and did not answer, he ordered these four soldiers to fire. The two companies of grenadiers, several of whom sprang to their arms, fired on this column. This brigade, caught in the disorder I have spoken of, some unarmed, others with their weapons, most of them in shirts, all fled to the path they had entered the woods. No sooner were they on the little plain that we have spoken of and where we had spent the night, when they saw cavalry coming towards them. Those closest jumped back into the wood; three or four hundred men threw themselves into the gap where the steep ground sheltered them from cavalry pursuit ... The Hanoverian column found no other resistance from this disorderly brigade, except a portion of two grenadier companies of the Régiment d'Enghien which had placed themselves in a kind of funnel formed by the ground where they held firm; but their whole brigade was in flight and they were all killed or captured there; the two *capitaines* were killed there: one named Saint-Pons and the other Miraval, from Aix-en-Provence.[40] This *regiment* lost another captain, wounded in the arm, named Grandvillars.[41, 42]

A little under a thousand strong, the d'Eu Brigade formed in haste and the Comte de Lorges attempted a manoeuvre he had no time to make. The brigade was knocked down the southern slope of the mountain. They lost many people to the fire of the enemy which plunged down, hitting the heads of the French. The Marquis d'Armentières' column in turn came under fire from the three Hanoverian battalions:

> The musket shots which fell on them also fell on the Imperial brigade, which also fired at Enghien. The fire was so intense that the Imperials were obliged to withdraw; the same fire also fell on the Swiss, who after a discharge withdrew. Alsace suffered the same fire without returning fire and reached the ravine. The *regiment* suffered greatly and fired; the Régiment de Belzunce, which was to the left of Champagne on the plain, did not fire. And so all this is what confused our troops in the woods.[43]

---

38   Sylvain Joseph Delmas, chevalier de Grammont (1748-1809). Began as an *enseigne* in the Régiment d'Enghien and became *lieutenant* in 1756. He was wounded in the shoulder and head at Hastenbeck. He became *capitaine* commander of the *colonel*'s company in 1771 then *capitaine de grenadiers* in 1779 and became *colonel* of the Régiment d'Enghien in 1791, which would become the 93e Régiment de Ligne.

39   Reding and Salis were Swiss regiments in the service of France and were dressed in red with blue cuffs and turnbacks and waistcoats; the three Hanoverian regiments wore red coats with white, yellow, or orange facings, lapels, and collars and their grenadiers wore the German 'mitre' cap.

40   François Louis Rigolet de Saint-Pons started as an *enseigne* in the Régiment d'Enghien in 1734, *lieutenant* in 1737, and *capitaine* from 1739. Félix Louis François d'Orcin de Miraval, *capitaine*, was born in 1731.

41   De Grandvillars was *lieutenant en second* in the Régiment d'Enghien in 1744, *capitaine* in 1748. His arm was broken by a musket shot.

42   Vogüé & Sourd, *Campagnes de Mercoyrol de Beaulieu*, pp.146-148.

43   Letter of an un-named officer, presumably from the Brigade de La Couronne, in Duc de Luynes, *Memoire du duc de Luynes*, Vol.XVI, p.132.

As Chapotte wrote, 'several columns entered the woods, climbed to the top of the mountain and fired on the enemy and sometimes on each other.'[44] The brigade of La Couronne, commanded by the Comte de Mailly, lost many men and one of its companies of grenadiers was decimated: they delivered a sharp fire to the Hanoverians but suffered for it, losing *Lieutenant* de Miègeville a *volontaire* named de la Rocque , and 20 men killed. Due to the masking terrain and vegetation, the red uniforms of the two Swiss regiments and the element of surprise, certain regiments fired at each other, especially on the Brigade d'Eu.

The Duc d'Orléans was in the second line with the cavalry he was preparing to advance to the centre. He was the first to notice the disorder and dispatched the Carabiniers to face Hastenbeck. Believing there were enough troops on that side, he then sent for the Comte de Maillebois from the left wing where the *Maréchal* had sent him to watch the manoeuvres at the time of the assault on the redoubt. When 'M. Donezan,'[45] aide-de-camp to the Duc d'Orléans,

> [H]ad led M. de Maillebois to the M. le Duc d'Orléans, and the prince explained the reason he had sent to seek him, M. de Maillebois said to him in clear terms, "this is a failed affair, there is still a column of the enemies which crossed the Weser, and which is moving on the camp of the Duc de Broglie; we have no choice but to withdraw." On this the Duc d'Orléans appeared to doubt the truth of these facts.[46]

Believing himself flanked, the Comte de Maillebois sent one of his *aide-marshal des logis*, the Chevalier de Puységur, to the redoubt below the woods where *Maréchal* d'Estrées was waiting for the dispatch, as a matter of urgency, from the two infantry and cavalry brigades near the Voremberg gap which linked to the Hanover road.[47] At the same time, without authorisation, Maillebois asked the Duc de Broglie to send his cavalry to contain the enemy at the foot of the gap on the right and fall back to the Hagenohsen defile along the Weser as was prescribed in the event of the army having to fall back. The Duc obeyed with the cavalry for which he had no immediate use but sent an officer to *Maréchal* d'Estrées to confirm the order to withdraw his infantry which had already crossed the Hastenbeck stream and was advancing on the Schmiedebrink, noting that the enemy was withdrawing before them. Faced with the hesitation of the Duc de Broglie, the Comte de Maillebois went to find the Marquis de Souvré in command in the second line on the far left and sent him to the Hagenohsen defile with the Palatine brigade.

---

44 Chapotte, *Sous Louis le Bien-Aimé*, p.79.
45 Presumably Charles Armand d'Usson de Bonnac, marquis de Donezan.
46 *Maréchal* d'Estrées, *Éclaircissements préséntes au roi*, p.45.
47 Barthélémy Athanase Herculin Chastenet, chevalier, then vicomte de Puységur (1719-1803) was *capitaine* in the Royal-Comtois. He was wounded in the expedition to Minorca under *Maréchal* de Richelieu in 1756 then became *aide du major-général (surnuméraire) de l'infanterie de l'armée du bas Rhin* in March 1757. He became *colonel* of a regiment of Grenadiers Royaux in 1761 and *maréchal de camp* in 1780.

Meanwhile, on the Obensburg, Mercoyrol de Beualieu wrote that the enemy column

> [H]ad seized the summit of the mountain where M. de Chevert had left M. de Randan, *lieutenant-général*, in command of the brigade d'Eu, the four cannon of the brigade d'Eu and the four of La Marine remained ill-timed, as has been said … The Hanoverian column, found these eight guns on the summit, and turned them on the French army on the plain at the bottom of the mountain.[48]

It was almost noon. These events had taken place in the three quarters of an hour since the capture of the redoubt by the Régiment de Champagne.

The eight regimental guns of the brigades d'Eu and La Marine at the top of the Obensburg were captured by the enemy and immediately aimed towards the right flank of the French army, in particular the squadrons of the Carabiniers who had advanced in front of Hastenbeck, at the foot of the mountain. They suffered from several volleys aimed directly at them.

Maréchal d'Estrées, still at the redoubt, received 'several different notices [which] came to him from different places at the same time'. The opinions were contradictory. Relying on his *maréchal general des logis*, he ordered the Lyonnais Brigade and the Carabiniers to move to the right as the Comte de Maillebois had asked him through the Chevalier de Puységur. The Carabiniers were almost there already, having just come under fire from the guns taken by the enemy on the Obensburg.

Initially the *Maréchal* believed the fire was a mistake and began by ordering a recall to the right to be beaten:

> Convinced that our troops had misunderstood and were firing at each other, I wanted to put an end to this error by ordering the drummers at the edge of the wood to sound the recall; but it was in vain. It was really the fire of enemy, and I'll admit I was worried about it. It had increased by eight guns the enemy had seized and which fired at the Carabiniers placed parallel to the ravine of Hastenbeck. I was too close to this event not to distinguish it.[49]

Pressed on all sides to make decisions, the *Maréchal* then gathered all the information that had come to him, events caused directly or indirectly from the action of the Comte de Maillebois losing his temper. As he later explained:

> At the same time M. le Duc de Broglie sent word to me that M. le Duc d´Orléans had sent him an order to march and begged me to tell him what he should do; my response was that he must obey the prince who apparently had seen urgent things that were unknown to me. A moment later I saw almost all the cavalry on my left scrambling to my right; I got other notices saying that the La Marine Brigade had lost its guns, that the Austrian troops had suffered greatly. All these events were reported to me in less than five minutes.[50]

---

48 Vogüe & Sourd, *Campagnes de Mercoyrol de Beaulieu*, p.148.
49 *Maréchal* d'Estrées, *Éclaircissements présentes au roi*, p.27.
50 *Maréchal* d'Estrées, *Éclaircissements présentes au roi*, pp.28-29.

An advantage offered itself on the plain in front of the *Maréchal* as he noted the enemy had retreated but hesitated to pursue this clear opportunity. 'After a few minutes M. de Chevert advised me that the enemies were withdrawing, and I could clearly see that there were only a few small cavalry troops left on the ground where the enemy army had been in line.'[51] The French infantry attacking at Hastenbeck in the centre of the line no longer had any opposition and could see only the Hessian and Hanoverian cavalry as an apparent rearguard. There was no direct news from Chevert's column which, having to descend from the heights, had not yet come into the open, but 'for officers who had the intelligence of war',[52] it was evident that the columns marching towards the Hanoverian centre and left had made them feel cut-off and concerned with being taken in flank by Chevert's victorious column and so the enemy had withdrawn.

However, some on the French side were surprised at such easy success against an opponent who had retreated so quickly. The cannon which thundered on the heights where Chevert was victorious an hour earlier was a signal to them of a return to the offensive by an enemy who had simulated giving ground on the left, and would return in force with an army corps to take the French army from the rear.

The attacks of von Breidenbach and Dachenhausen's three battalions and six squadrons was to have immense consequences: *Maréchal* d'Estrées was mistaken about the seriousness of the disorder on his right and wished to guard against what he believed to be a more dangerous attack. He ordered forward movement to be halted and made defensive arrangements to the rear at the very moment he saw part of his left wing cavalry pass at a great trot, heading towards the Voremberg gap on the right in all haste. As he later wrote:

> All these events were reported to me in less than five minutes and gave me the idea to change my position, or retire if I had to, or to put myself in a position to march to the enemies if they came in force on my right flank … I said: "M. de Puységur, have we thought about our *équipages*? They need to pass beyond the Halle defiles." To which he responded: "In these circumstances we need orders in writing." "You write them," I told him, "and I will sign them." From that moment I was busy getting the artillery and all the infantry to return through Hastenbeck ravine, except for Champagne and the Grenadiers de France; I sent word to M. de Chevert to withdraw on me. The more he warned me that there were hardly any troops in front of him, the more they had disappeared from my eyes in favour of the woods and the mountains, the more I was persuaded by the movements which were made behind me that the enemy was moving on our right flank on the Hanover road.[53]

This change of the French position strongly resembled a retreat. Despite the advice of some of his staff officers and generals commanding the attack

---

51   *Maréchal* d'Estrées, *Éclaircissements présentes au roi*, pp.27.
52   Rousset, *Le comte de Gisors*, p.227.
53   *Maréchal* d'Estrées, *Éclaircissements présentes au roi*, pp.29-30.

columns, the *Maréchal* gave orders for a partial retreat, beyond the stream and the ravine:

> At the first order I gave, several people, MM. de Guerchy, Cornillon, Chabo, and many others came to me to make representations dictated to them by their zeal for the service of the King and by their friendship for me; since they were all unaware of the different advice I had received, they were naturally surprised at my resolve. I ordered, however, as one who wished to be obeyed. The infantry crossed [back over] the Hastenbeck ravine; I lined it with artillery; I sent d'Eu Brigade to the mouth of the gorge; I wanted to give the same order to the Palatines; but M. de Souvré, who was at their head, did not receive it: he had already marched back to take these same posts, which I did not know until long after the battle.[54]

Indeed, the Marquis de Souvré had already marched on Hagenohsen on the orders of the Comte de Maillebois. Some cavalry squadrons which had remained on the left wing and were advancing to start the pursuit were even stopped by a general who 'personally carried the fatal order to the Royal-Pologne cavalry brigade, which enclosed the left of the plain and had come forward to take advantage of the disorder of the routed army: this same officer stopped them despite what he saw'.[55] As Chapotte put it:

> The *Maréchal* believed himself lost, he ordered a retreat, he sent all the light troops to his rear to protect the *équipages* to whom he sent orders to flee; the whole army, in spite of itself, was forced to obey its general, and made a retrograde move; the valets, *vivandiers*, surgeons who were spectators were taken by dread.[56]

The *équipages* flew to the rear so quickly that part of the army thought the battle was lost, as Valfons recorded: 'There was a faked order to increase the camp escort by fifteen hundred horses; but fortunately Chabo, *maréchal des logis de la cavalerie*, found the ordnance rider who carried this order, arrested him, and upon verification, M. d'Estrées denied having given it.'[57]

This pause caused by the French flustering allowed the Duke of Cumberland to retreat with his artillery without being pursued and incurring additional casualties. After firing his captured guns from the Obensburg, *Oberst* von Breidenbach, 'seeing his entire army in full retreat, made his own, taking the eight guns with him: one was dismounted and its wheels broken; the enemy abandoned it and it was found the next day, covered with branches.'[58]

Chevert had descended from the Obensburg woods to take the Hanoverian army in the flank. He marched with the Régiment de Picardie at the front, followed by Navarre, then most of La Marine. Leaving the enemy to withdraw to his right towards Hameln and without fear of the fire which he heard behind him on the left, he finally emerged onto the plain above

---

54 Maréchal d'Estrées, *Éclaircissements présentés au roi*, p.31.
55 Valfons, *Souvenirs du marquis de Valfons*, p.276.
56 Chapotte, *Sous Louis le Bien-Aimé*, p.79.
57 Valfons, *Souvenirs du marquis de Valfons*, p.277.
58 Vogüé & Sourd, *Campagnes de Mercoyrol de Beaulieu*, p.148.

Hastenbeck. 'Arriving at the woods' edge behind the enemy; we were very surprised to see the enemy army in full retreat and already out of range of our cannon. Masters of the battlefield, we saw French troops had just made a retrograde march which moved them away from the said battlefield.'[59]

Noting the enemy's withdrawal, Chevert sent representations to *Maréchal* d'Estrées not to withdraw as requested which would allow victory to slip away. Other officers including the Marquis de Cornillon, *major general de l'infanterie*, and the Marquis de Vogüé, agreed with this. The Comte de Guerchy at the head of the Grenadiers de France seeing the enemy retreat, refused to carry out the withdrawal order and sent the Marquis de Saint-Pern with a brigade of Grenadiers de France in pursuit of the enemy. Finally, the Chevalier de Chabo, *maréchal general des logis de la cavalerie*, who returned from his reconnaissance of the gap, announced that there was neither cavalry nor infantry in the woods. The Duke of Cumberland had not made any bypassing manoeuvre or left a full corps or even a division.

One hour after Chevert's column had emerged from the woods, the Duc de Broglie finally noted that the withdrawal was unnecessary and gave the order to the rest of the Grenadiers de France to continue forward and engaged the Carabiniers and the Royal-Pologne cavalry, on the plain under the orders of the Duke of Fitzjames, to do the same. However, the enemy had already retreated out of reach behind the stream where the Hameln River began. The Duc stopped the pursuit and occupied Afferde. The Hastenbeck woods were held by the Grenadiers de France supported by the Régiments de Picardie and Champagne, while the cavalry formed on the plain in line to the left of the infantry. The troops, who had been under arms for three days, rested wearily in this safe and convenient position.

It was 4:00 p.m. and the battle was over for want of an adversary. Slowly it became apparent that the French had been victorious, as Chapotte wrote:

> We started to hope we weren't beaten and a few hours later everyone was saying to themselves, "I think we won the battle!" There were still unbelievers by nightfall. However, it is very certain that we held the enemy's battlefield in the evening, although we had retreated from our [position] at the same time as they left theirs; the main body of our army never made its retreat beyond the woods, and I saw part of the enemy force withdrawing before Hameln which they left on their left, and part towards Hanover before dark, and they were already very far away when nightfall hid them from me.
>
> It must be well judged that an army which wins a battle the very moment it withdraws and believes itself beaten does not pursue the enemy; they were indeed allowed to go very peacefully; they left four guns which they could not remove, the carriages of most being broken; they perhaps took some of our own [guns] that were said to be lost in the woods and that have apparently been searched for and found; they did not lose any colours or standards and we had some colours lost in the woods; they lost a thousand to twelve hundred men and we lost two thousand; yet this action, such as it is, does a great deal of honour to the worth of

---

[59] Vogüé & Sourd, *Campagnes de Mercoyrol de Beaulieu*, pp.149-150.

the nation; every other army perished in these sharp gorges and could not pass, it took incredible bravery and audacity to pierce this passage and it was foolish to hope to end with an army more numerous than ours: The Duke of Cumberland was so certain of stopping and destroying us that all the country beyond this point had the utmost confidence in his word.[60]

Nevertheless, he felt that the fruits of victory were small: 'We took very few prisoners, took few standards or colours and few cannon, and I saw that the pursuit would not do any great harm to the enemy'.[61] Another account is more positive:

> The victory was not bloody, but it secured operations for the rest of the campaign. One cannot deny that M. le *Maréchal*'s dispositions were very good. Moreover, the whole army and M. le *Maréchal* himself attributed [victory] to M. de Vallière, who extended the success of the day to the Corps Royal [de la Artillerie] ... As the *Maréchal* passed the artillery on his way back from the battlefield, the soldiers of the Corps Royal shouted for joy over his victory. "You won it well," he told them, "you won it well!"[62]

The French took nine large calibre cannon and two howitzers from the redoubt as well as 15 ammunition boxes but lost the eight regimental pieces left on the Obensburg, of which only six were removed by the enemy. The other two were discarded after being rendered unusable.

The battle was fought by manoeuvre and the lines hardly fired at all. Although accompanied by fire from the grenadiers placed at the front, the French columns marched mainly with bayonets:

> The regiments which charged were the two Austrians, Picardie, Champagne, Navarre, La Marine, Belzunce, Alsace, Saint-Germain, Eu, Enghien, Salis-Suisse. Of all of them, only the Austrians, Champagne and d'Eu's brigade fired: the others, including Conti and La Couronne, fixed bayonets at the end of the musket without firing a single shot; the enemies fled first after giving their fire.[63]

In total, nearly 3,000 men remained on the battlefield, killed or wounded. On the French side, official losses amounted to 1,055 killed (including 17 officers) and 1,277 wounded.[64] Half these losses were from Chevert's column, some of whose soldiers were not recovered until the evening or the following day due to the topography of the battlefield around the Scheckenberg. Valfons wrote that:

---

60 Chapotte, *Sous Louis le Bien-Aimé*, pp.80-81.
61 Chapotte, *Sous Louis le Bien-Aimé*, p.68.
62 Letter, 27 July 1757, from the battlefield near Hamelm in Duc de Luynes, *Memoires du duc de Luynes*, Vol.XVI, p.130.
63 Tourny to his father in Duteil, *Une famille militaire au XVIIIe siècle*, p.469.
64 *Gazette*, no. 33 13 août 1757. See Appendix VII.

I occupied myself for three days traversing all the winding paths and ravines of the wood where we had fought, to have the dead buried and look for the wounded who had remained there without help; I was fortunate enough to see my attention rewarded, saving many Hanoverians, Hessians and French who continued their lives because of my zeal, having wished only to bring them back was to me a most precious duty.[65]

As for the losses of the Hanoverian army, the report of the Duke of Cumberland announced 357 killed (including 36 officers), 910 wounded (including 106 officers) and 213 prisoners (including 4 officers).[66]

With the Hanoverian army withdrawn, even with few casualties, victory belonged to the French. For *Maréchal* d'Estrées, the lack of coordination of the French command, the greater losses suffered, and the enemy's withdrawal in good order, the Battle of Hastenbeck only offered a military victory; honourable but incomplete. Nonetheless, the consequences of the battle would have a decisive impact on the strategic plan.

---

65 Marquis de Valfons, *Souvenirs du marquis de Valfons*, p.279.
66 Waddington, *La guerre de sept ans*, p.444.

Epilogue

> M. le Maréchal d'Estrées ... had the sad experience, from beginning of the 1757 campaign, of a general who lacked the most important things for the good of the army which became useless in the service of the King and ran the risk of losing his honour and his reputation, because of continual accusations of blindness or not doing what would have been impossible.[1]

Blaming himself for having taken the alarm too lightly following the first French successes on his left, the Duke of Cumberland fell prey to a form of apathy. Deaf to the requests of the Duke of Brunswick and several other general officers of his staff, and against the orders he himself had given before the battle, he continued with his army to march on Minden rather than hold at Hameln.

On 27 July, the day after the battle, *Maréchal* d'Estrées sent the Duc de Fitzjames with a detachment of 600 cavalry and 12 companies of grenadiers, supported by the Grenadiers de France, to make contact with the enemy army. The Duc moved to Hessisch-Oldendorf, north-west of Hameln along the Weser, and could not help but observe the retreat of the Hanoverian army on Minden.

The Grenadiers de France, on the right bank of the Weser, and the corps of the Duc de Broglie, on the left, began to invest the area around Hameln to begin the siege. After an initial rejection, the garrison asked to surrender the following day. Preferring to rest the entire army while taking a few days from the rest of the campaign, *Maréchal* d'Estrées accepted *Generalmajor* Brunck's terms. The garrison of 700 men would leave with the honours of the war on 30 July, to be taken to Hanover with horses and crews but without artillery. Militiamen and invalids would be sent home on condition that they would no longer serve until the end of the war, but the 800 wounded and sick of the Duke of Cumberland's army also in town would remain prisoners of war, including *Generalmajor* Hodemberg.

While the Duke of Cumberland continued his flight in the direction of Nienburg, Hameln opened its gates to 20 companies of French grenadiers on

---

1 Duc de Luynes, *Memoires du duc de Luynes*, Vol.XVI, pp.485-486.

EPILOGUE

'His Royal Highness William Augustus Duke of Cumberland &c. &c.'. Hand-coloured engraving by Lempereur after Morier, published June 30, 1751. (Anne S.K. Brown Collection)

28 July, at 4:00 p.m. who were the first to occupy the town. The garrison left on the 30th, as agreed, in good order. The French army set up its ovens and hospitals in the town but camped in Hessisch-Oldendorf.

Multiple accounts recorded the occupation of the town and the booty that was found within its walls:

> Fifty-four guns of cast-iron, nineteen of iron were found at Hameln; ten cast-iron mortars; three howitzers; twenty-eight thousand balls; four thousand bombs; two thousand muskets; one hundred and fifty-five thousand [*livres*] powder; two hundred thousand *livres* of lead and boats intended to form a Bridge over the Weser.[2]

> This city was of considerable resource to us with its stores of fodder, all kinds of grain and abundance of wine, thirty-six cannon of all calibres, but mainly siege guns … The army stayed two days at Hameln, where its *équipages* joined them; on the third, they set out after the enemy. The next day, they took a second march, then took a rest.[3]

> It was M. le Comte de Gisors, *colonel* of Champagne and son of the *Maréchal* de Belle-Isle, who carried the news to the King, and M. de Montmirail, nephew of M. d'Estrées, that of the capture of Hameln. The war would have ended that day if the operation of M. d'Estrées had not been disturbed. On 30 July, at seven o'clock in the evening, M. le *Maréchal* received orders to be recalled, and learned that M. de Richelieu had come to replace him: let us judge by his regrets and those of the army![4]

In the aftermath of the capture of Hameln, the Hanoverian army at Loccum continued to retreat north from the Hanover electorate through Nienburg, Kloster-Zeven, and Stade. The French army manoeuvred to cut their lines of communication; the Duc de Randan's reserve was at Bisperode and the Duc of Broglie's was at Hameln on the left bank of the Weser. It was at this point that the King made the decision to give command of the army to the Duc de Richelieu.

The courier dismissing *Maréchal* d'Estrées had left on 25 July. The secret of the news had been well kept until then and only nine people had known. Seven, including *Maréchal* Richelieu and the Marquise de Pompadour, were at court with the King. The eighth, alone, was in the army in the person of the Comte de Maillebois, who, informed by a letter from the Minister, his father-in-law, sent on 2 July and received by the 7th. While he was winning the Battle of Hastenbeck, *Maréchal* d'Estrées was no longer commander-in-chief of his army. The news of his replacement and his victory crossed paths and reached their destination almost simultaneously.

The orders insinuated that the *Maréchal* d'Estrées, 'would do well to serve with M. de Richelieu who is his senior. His father-in-law and his friends would also give him advice', to claim that he was returning to France for the

---

2 *Gazette*, no. 33, 13 août 1757.
3 Vogüé & Sourd, *Campagnes de Mercoyrol de Beaulieu*, p.150.
4 Valfons, *Souvenirs du marquis de Valfons*, p.279.

sake of his health.⁵ Despite this he personally informed his staff that the King was withdrawing his command.

> There was grumbling in Paris of the time it had taken to conquer the Electorate of Hanover; it was not understood why he was not already on the ramparts of Magdeburg. But people were willing to forget that, in the space of three months, he had penetrated from the banks of the Rhine to the gates of Hanover, conquered East Frisia, occupied Bremen, subjugated Hesse and left the Allies out of position to offer subsequent resistance. There was a feigned ignorance that a general leading a French army in Germany must think of the means of providing for his subsistence, and of securing his retirement, in case of misfortune. An army general is to be pitied, when his merit does not serve as an umbrella against the poisonous features of the base schemers who besiege the throne of an indolent and characterless monarch!⁶

Chapotte wrote positively of the change:

> *Maréchal* Richelieu arrived yesterday, he took command of the army from *Maréchal* d'Estrées who will leave in a few days. The army is lacking everything, for this reason it marauds excessively; famine causes marauding and marauding increases famine; *Maréchal* Richelieu announced that this will change, he has already spoken very firmly to the *intendant*, threatened the provosts, contractors and clerks and greatly embraced the troops: It is the rising of the sun.⁷

Mercoyrol de Beaulieu, on the other hand, remarked that the change was regretted:

> The army was astonished to be informed that *Maréchal* de Richelieu had arrived [on 3 August] to take command of the army, which *Maréchal* d'Estrées was to cede to him by leaving immediately for Versailles [on 7 August]. The army very much regretted *Maréchal* d'Estrées; they could not get used to the idea that he was removed from his position at the moment he had just won a battle which gave him the conquest of the entire Electorate of Hanover, and it was said, "Ah well, he's leaving covered with laurels and, arriving with them at Versailles, the Minister and the King will be very sorry for such a blunder", which consoled them for the injustice experienced by their general.⁸

This view that the change was ill-timed was not unique:

> *Maréchal* Richelieu arrives here at a singular moment, a battle won, a country conquered. It is disagreeable to replace a general so favoured in war and so unfavoured at court; besides, apart from driving out the enemy at Nienburg,

---

5   Letter from the court to Compiègne, 28 July 1757 in Duc de Luynes, *Memoires du duc de Luynes*, Vol.XVI, p.121.
6   De Retzow, *Nouveaux mémoires historiques sur la guerre de Sept ans*, p.220.
7   Chapotte, *Sous Louis le Bien-Aimé*, p.82.
8   Vogüé & Sourd, *Campagnes de Mercoyrol de Beaulieu*, p.151.

there is nothing left to do but to establish winter quarters because the army has marched so far and become so tired that diseases are starting to become common, and the battalions are shrinking before one's eyes. The horses of the cavalry and of the dragoons are skeletons and they die daily. Truthfully, it [the army] has to get to Dampierre since it cannot get to Compiègne. We are still staying here, where we proceed to enter the houses whose keys are brought to us and knock on doors of those which are closed to us. That will result in more marches which will occupy the six weeks or two months during which one can move about in this country, after which it will be the most perfect quagmire through winter. If the army remained in the indolence they said it was, I would have been able to give you news from my hand sooner, but we have always been in the air; the marches, my service, the burdens of the company, did not leave the possibility.[9]

Chapotte developed his theme with a comparison of the two commanders:

Maréchal Richelieu coddles the troops a lot, promising them good winter treatment, and he is loved without having done anything yet, while *Maréchal* d'Estrées, scornful of everyone, is totally forgotten despite the day of the 26 July, which allowed the entire conquest of this country. One man has a lot of wit and moulds his character on the minds of the men he commands, the other has less wit, more stubbornness of character and no knowledge of men; the spirit and flexibility of one will sincerely attach many skilled soldiers to him, will listen to the advice he is given and make him decide what is best; the stubborn and presumptuous mind of the other will put off everyone, he will listen to any kind of advice, and he will remain too weak to follow a good course on his own. An army in which there will be able people will necessarily be happy under the orders of *Maréchal* Richelieu; under the orders of *Maréchal* d'Estrées, eight to ten thousand men may be able to make some brilliant strike, but a larger army will not succeed, in other areas the balance is equal between these two *maréchaux* in their other qualities as citizens and generals.[10]

The French army soon occupied the entire Electorate of Hanover, taking Hameln on 28 July, Minden on 1 August and Hanover on the 3rd. Hesse-Cassel, Brunswick, Hanover, and the Duchies of Bremen and Verden were made to pay contributions.

On 9 September, *Maréchal* Richelieu and the Duke of Cumberland signed a convention at Kloster-Zeven, 100 kilometres from Hamburg. The French army occupied the entire Electorate of Hanover. The Brunswick and Hessian troops returned home, unarmed and without prisoners. The Hanoverian troops were sent to the Duchy of Lauenburg, on the right bank of the Elbe.

---

9   Letter from the camp at Oldendorf, 5 August 1757 in Duc de Luynes, *Memoires du duc de Luynes*, Vol.XVI, pp.300-301.
10 Chapotte, *Sous Louis le Bien-Aimé*, p.82.

EPILOGUE

The French military terms of the Kloster-Zeven convention have been widely criticised because the Duke of Cumberland had no other way out than surrender. *Maréchal* Richelieu could have destroyed the Hanoverian army or taken it prisoner, he made 'the fault of not disarming and dismissing the Hanoverian troops'.[11] As Jomini later put it, 'we soon had cause to repent of the lightness with which we let them go'.[12]

---

11 Napoleon I, *Précis dés guerres de Frédéric II*, p.43.
12 Baron Antoine Henri de Jomini, *Histoire ciritque et militaire des guerres de Frédéric II* (Brussels: J. P. Moens, 1874), p.75.

Appendix I

Order of Battle of the Armée du Bas Rhin

M. LE *MARÉCHAL* D'ESTRÉES

ÉTAT-MAJOR
Comte de Maillebois, *maréchal général des logis de le armeé*
Prince de Turenne, *colonel général commandant la cavalerie*
Duc de Chevreuse, *colonel général commandant les dragons*
Duc de Coigny, *mestre de camp général*
Marquis de Cornillon, *major-général de l'infanterie*
Chevalier de Chabo, *maréchal général des logis de la cavalerie*

FIRST LINE

Lieutenants-Généraux
Duc d'Orléans, Marquis de Villemur, Comte de Bercheny.
Duc de Chaulnes, Chevalier de Muy, Duc de Fitzjames, Comte de Courten, Comte de Noailles, Comte de la Vauguyon, Comte de Guerchy, Marquis de Souvré, Duc d'Ayen, Marquis du Poulpry, Comte de Sourches.

Maréchaux de Camp
Comte de Vauban, Marquis de Lastic, Marquis de Barbançon, Marquis de Brancas, Marquis de Fouquet, Comte du Rumain, Marquis de Péreuse, Marquis de Dauvet, Duc de Laval, Chevalier de Maupeou, Marquis de Ségur, Duc d'Antin, Prince de Beauvau, Duc d'Olonne, Comte de Vence, Chevalier d'Ailly, Comte de Jonzac, Chevalier du Châtelet, Comte de la Guiche, Comte du Luc.

Infantry
The Brigade de Picardie held the left in the order of battle as the two Austrian battalions held the place of honour on the right. The French troops were considered auxiliaries to those of the Empress Queen of Hungary.

APPENDIX I

Brigades	Regiments	Battalions
Chevalier de Croismare (Le Roi)	Austrians	2
	La Marche	4
	Le Roi	4
Marquis de Chastelard (Gardes Lorraine)	Dauphin	2
	Gardes Lorraine	2
Chevalier de Rochechouart (Aquitaine)	Aquitaine	2
	Vastan	2
	Palatines	4
Marquis de Langeron (Condé)	Vaubécourt	2
	Condé	2
Marquis de La Roche-Aymon (La Roche-Aymon)	Lyonnais	2
	La Roche-Aymon	2
Marquis de Mailly	Mailly	4
Marquis de Bréhant (Picardie)	Chartres	2
	Picardie	4
Total		40

Cavalry

Brigades	Regiments	Squadrons
Right Wing		
Comte de Vienne (Clermont-Prince)	Colonel-Général	3
	Clermont-Prince	2
	Bourgogne	2
Comte de Galiffet (La Reine)	La Reine	2
	Bourbon-Busset	2
	Conti	2
M. de Sarlabout (Noailles)	Charost	2
	Noailles	2
	Royal-Cravates	2
Total		19
Left Wing		
Comte de Clermont-Tonnerre (Clermont-Tonnerre)	Royal Roussillon	2
	Fumel	2
	Clermont-Tonnerre	2
Comte de Périgord (Dauphin)	Talleyrand	2
	Moustier	2
	Dauphin	2
Marquis de Bellefonds (Bellefonds)	Aquitaine	2
	Bellefonds	2
	Commissaire-Général	2
Total		18

Dragoons

Lieutenants-Généraux
Prince de Beauffremont, Marquis de La Salle, Duc de Chevreuse, Marquis de La Suze, Marquis d'Armentiéres

Marechaux de Camp
Marquis de Champignelle, Marquis de Voyer, Marquis d'Escorailles, Comte de Raugrave, Chevalier de Pons, Marquis d'Asfeld.

Brigades	Regiments	Squadrons
Marquis de Goyon (Colonel-Général)	Le Roi	4
	Aubigné	4
	Colonel-Général	4
Comte de Lillebonne (d'Harcourt)	Orléans	4
	Harcourt	4
	Mestre-de-Camp	4
	Total	24

SECOND LINE

Lieutenants-Généraux
Duc de Brissac, Marquis de Contades, Duc de Randan.
Duc de Fleury, Comte de Montboissier, Marquis de Morangies, Comte de Fitzjames, Duc de Durat, Duc d'Havré, Duc de Lauraguais, M. de Chevert, Baron de Montmorency, Comte d'Andlau, Marquis de Fremur.

Maréchaux de Camp
Marquis de Montmort, Comte de Lutzelbourg, Comte de Verceil, Marquis de Ruffey, Comte de Sparre, Comte d'Orlick, M. de Planta, Comte de Bergeyck, Marquis de Leyde, Comte de la Massais, Marquis d'Escars, Comte de Montmorency, Comte de Beaucaire, Marquis de Saint-Simon, Marquis de la Cheze.

Infantry

Brigades	Regiments	Battalions
Comte de Polignac (Enghien)	Navarre	4
	Eu	2
	Enghien	2
Marquis de La Chatre (Cambrésis)	La Couronne	2
	Cambrésis	1
	Périgord	1
Chevalier de La Marck (La Marck)	La Marck	2
	Lowendahl	2

APPENDIX I

Baron de Tunderfeld (Royal-Suédois)	Palatines	4
	Royal-Suédois	2
	Royal-Bavière	2
Baron de Bergh (Bergh)	Bentheim	2
	Royal-Pologne	1
	Bergh	1
Marquis de Sailly (Conti)	Orléans	2
	Conti	2
Comte de Gisors (acting brigadier)	Champagne	4
Total		36

Cavalry

Brigades	Regiments	Squadrons
Right Wing		
Marquis d'Ecquevilly (Royal-Cavalerie)	Royal	2
	Archaic	2
	Berry	2
Marquis de Soyécourt (Dauphin-Étranger)	Dauphin-Étranger	2
	De Vienne	2
	Lusignan	2
Vicomte d'Escars (Escars)	Bourbon	2
	Escars	2
	Royal-Piémont	2
Total		18
Left Wing		
Marquis de Béthune (Royal-Pologne)	Royal-Pologne	2
	Harcourt	2
	Henrichemont	2
Chevalier de Fleury (Fleury)	Orléans	2
	Fleury	2
	Royal-Étranger	2
Total		12

Note: Some generals were transferred to the Armée du Haut Rhin under the *Maréchal* Duc de Richelieu: Comte de Noailles, Baron de Montmorency, Chevalier de Muy, Comte d'Andlau, Comte de la Vauguyon and Duc of Havré, *lieutenant-généraux*; M. de Planta, Marquis de Lastic, Comte de Lutzelbourg, Comte du Luc, Comte de Vence, Marquis de Voyer, Prince de Beauvau, Comte de la Guiche, *maréchaux de camp*.

ARTILLERY
M. de Valliére, *lieutenant-général*
Chevalier de Fontenay, *maréchal de camp*

Chevalier Despictières	La Motte	1 Company
	Menonville	1 Company
(90 guns)	Cosne	1 Company

HEAD-QUARTERS GUARDS
Marquis de Saint-Pern (*inspecteur-commandant des grenadiers de France*), *lieutenant-général*
Comte de Beausobre, Marquis de Dreux, *maréchaux de camp*

Brigades	Regiments	Battalions
Comte de Lanjamet	Grenadiers de France	4
Chevalier de Modéne	Grens. Royaux de Modéne	2
	Grens. Royaux de Chantilly	2
M. de Bergeret	Grens. Royaux d'Aulan	2
	Grens. Royaux de Bergeret	2
Total		12

DETACHED REGIMENTS

Infantry

Regiments	Battalions
Austrians	2
Jenner-Suisse	2
Courten-Suisse	2
Lochman-Suisse	2
Foix	1
Nassau-Sarrebruck	1
Nassau-Usingen	1
La Dauphine	1
Total	12

Cavalry

Regiments	Squadrons
Maugiron	2
Lenoncourt	2
Dampierre	2
Total	6

FORWARD CORPS

Grenadiers de Solar, Volontaires Royaux, Chasseurs de Fischer, Volontaires de Flandre, Volontaires de Hainaut.

HUSSARS

Brigade	Regiments	Squadrons
Comte de Turpin	Turpin	4
	Polleretsky	4
	Bercheny	4
Total		12

CARABINIERS[1]

Marechaux de camp

M. de La Valette, Marquis d'Estourmel, Marquis de Poyanne

Corps	Brigades	Squadrons
M. de Maisons	Maisons	2
	Bovet	2
	Durfort	2
	La Tour	2
	Saint-Georges	2
Total		10

RESERVE

Prince de Soubise

16 Battalions

24 Squadrons

10 Artillery Pieces

TOTALS

Infantry (Battalions)		105
Cavalry (Squadrons)	Cavalry	77
	Dragoons	24
	Hussars	12
	Reserve	24
	Detached	6
Artillery Pieces		90

---

1 The 10 squadrons of the Corps of Carabiniers were divided into five 'Brigades' of two squadrons each.

Appendix II

State of the Armée du Bas Rhin, 1 July 1757

Infantry

Bielefeld Camp		
Regiment	Subaltern officers present	Soldiers under arms present
Prince de Ligne (Austrian)	19	461
Saxe-Gotha (Austrian)	19	540
Picardie	137	2,231
Navarre	141	2,476
Champagne	142	2,447
La Marine	132	2,305
Mailly	144	2,416
Le Roi	230	2,642
Lyonnais	64	1,101
Dauphin	71	1,256
Vaubécourt	70	1,139
Aquitaine	67	1,257
Eu	69	1,223
Orléans	74	1,201
La Couronne	68	1,193
Gardes Lorraine	68	1,234
La Roche-Aymon	68	1,235
Condé	68	1,199
Grenadiers de France	140	2,077
Vastan	67	1,241
La Marck	70	1,128
Chartres	71	1,246
Conti	66	1,090
Enghien	68	1,023

APPENDIX II

Royal-Pologne	35	599
Grenadiers Royaux de Modéne	48	1,060
Grenadiers Royaux d'Aulan	50	940
La Motte – Artillerie	65	550
Menonville – Artillerie	37	454
	2,368	38,964

Marquis d'Armentiéres' Reserve		
Régiment	Subaltern officers present	Soldiers under arms present
Belzunce	138	2,188
Reding-Suisse	55	1,223
Alsace	91	1,676
Saint-Germain	30	512
Salis-Suisse	54	1,150
	368	6,749
Duc de Broglie's Reserve		
Régiment	Subaltern officers present	Soldiers under arms present
Poitou	71	1,112
Provence	71	1,142
Royal-Suédois	76	1,063
Royal-Bavière	72	1,266
	290	4,583

Dragoons

Regiment	Effectives under arms	Horses
Colonel-Général	590	602
Mestre-de-Camp-Général	583	627
Orléans	573	679
	1,746	1,908

Cavalry

Regiment	Effectives under arms	Horses
Colonel-Général	412	419
Mestre-de-Camp-Général	276	274
Royal	274	280
Le Roi	275	279
Cuirassiers	277	278
Royal-Cravates	271	276
Royal-Roussillon	269	280

Royal-Allemand	280	280
Carabiniers-Maisons	267	279
Carabiniers-Saint-Georges	269	272
Carabiniers-Bovet	260	273
Royal-Pologne	277	278
Dauphin	275	280
Bourgogne	278	277
Aquitaine	242	242
Berry	274	274
Orléans	200	214
Condé	277	278
Bourbon	274	279
Marcieu	272	277
Talleyrand	269	280
Clermont-Tonnerre	245	245
Charost	244	244
Beauvilliers	279	279
Bourbon-Busset	270	274
Maugiron	237	245
Fumel	275	277
La Rochefoucault	272	280
De Vienne	240	245
Lameth	278	279
Lenoncourt	241	244
Bellefonds	274	280
Dampierre	275	274
Henrichemont	274	280
Moustier	278	279
Saluces	274	280
Noailles	262	272
Wurtemberg	277	279
d'Harcourt	271	276
Nassau	280	280
	11,094	11,254

Appendix III

Maréchal d'Estrées' Camp at Frenke on 24 & 25 July 1757

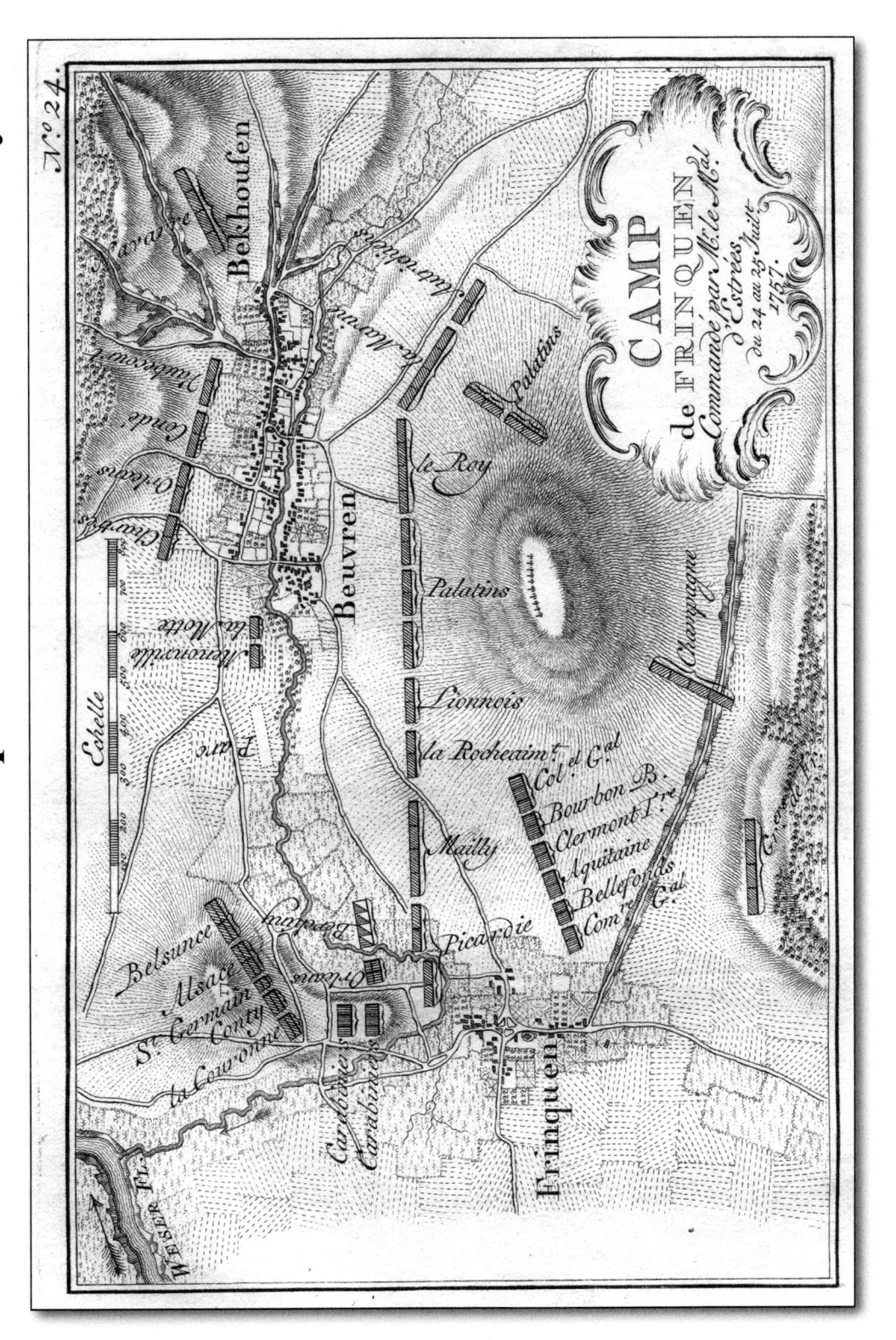

Appendix IV

Battle of Hastenbeck 26 July 1757: Order of Battle of the Infantry of *Maréchal* d'Estrées' Armée du Bas Rhin

Far Right: M. de Chevert, *lieutenant-général*	
Marquis de Vogüé and Chevalier de Maupeou, *maréchaux de camp.*	
Volontaires du Hainaut	350 men*
Volontaires de Flandre	350 men
Brigade de Picardie	4 Battalions
Brigade de Navarre	4 Battalions
Brigade de La Marine	4 Battalions
Grenadiers from the 12 battalions	12 Companies
Reserve Right: Duc de Randan, *lieutenant-général*	
Comte de Lorges, *maréchal de camp.*	
Régiment d'Eu	2 Battalions
Régiment d'Enghien	2 Battalions
Right Wing: Marquis d'Armentiéres, *lieutenant-général*	
Comte de Mailly and Duc de Chevreuse, *lieutenant-généraux*	
Prince de Ligne (Austrian)	1 Battalions
Saxe-Gotha (Austrian)	1 Battalions
Austrian Grenadiers	4 Companies
Régiment de Belzunce	4 Battalions
Régiment de La Couronne	2 Battalions
Régiment de Conti	2 Battalions
Régiment d'Alsace	3 Battalions
Régiment Saint-Germain	1 Battalions
Dragons Colonel-Général**	4 Squadrons

Dragons Mestre-de-Camp-Général	4 Squadrons
Dragons d'Orléans	4 Squadrons
Reserve Centre: Marquis d'Anlézy, *lieutenant-général*	
Régiment de Champagne	4 Battalions
Régiment de Reding-Suisse	2 Battalions
Régiment de Salis-Suisse	2 Battalions
Centre: Marquis de Contades, *lieutenant-général*	
Régiment du Roi	4 Battalions
Régiment de Mailly	4 Battalions
Régiment de Vaubécourt	2 Battalions
Régiment de Condé	2 Battalions
Régiment d'Orléans	2 Battalions
Régiment de Chartres	2 Battalions
Régiment Lyonnais	2 Battalions
Régiment La Roche Aymon	2 Battalions
Comte de Guerchy, *lieutenant-général*, and Marquis de Saint-Pern, *lieutenant-général*, commander of the Grenadiers de France	
Grenadiers Royaux de Solar	2 Battalions
Grenadiers de France	4 Battalions
Left Wing: Duc de Broglie, *lieutenant-général*	
Régiment de Lyonnais	2 Battalions
Régiment de Provence	2 Battalions
Régiment Royal-Suédois	2 Battalions
Régiment Royal-Baviére	2 Battalions
Second Line: Marquis de Souvré, *lieutenant-général*	
Baron d'Iselbach, *Generalmajor*, commander of the two Palatine brigades	
Regiment von der Osten	2 Battalions
Regiment Prinz von Zweibrucken	2 Battalions
Regiment von Preysing	2 Battalions
Regiment von Baaden	2 Battalions
Regiment Prinz Birkenfeld	2 Battalions

*In theory the full strength of the Volontaires de Flandre and Hainaut was six companies, of 40 infantry and 30 cavalry each, for an estimated total 200 foot and 150 horse on 26 July.

** These three regiments of dragoons were on foot and in the second line.

Appendix V

Battle of Hastenbeck 26 July 1757: Order of Battle of the Duke of Cumberland's Left Wing of the Army of Observation

Vanguard of the Left Wing, guarding the batteries	
Major von Freytag, commander of the detachment in the Obensburg Woods	
Hanoverian Jäger	3 Companies
Generalmajor von Schulenburg, commanding a brigade of grenadiers protecting the battery furthest east before Voremberg.	
Brunswick Grenadiers	1 Battalion
Hesse Grenadiers	1 Battalion
Hanover Grenadiers	1 Battalion
Generalmajor von Hardenberg, commanding a brigade of grenadiers from the second line which fought to reinforce the grenadiers attacked in the woods.	
Hanover Grenadiers	2 Battalions
Hesse Grenadiers	1 Battalion
Brunswick Grenadiers	1 Battalion
Left Wing: *Generalleutnant* von Imhoff	
Generalmajor von Behr, commanding a brigade guarding the redoubt batteries.	
Hanoverian Regiment Block	1 Battalion
Hanoverian Regiment Bruck	1 Battalion
Brunswick Regiment Imhoff	2 Battalions

APPENDIX V

Brunswick Regiment Zastrow	1 Battalion

Erbprinz of Brunswick, commanding a Brunswick brigade behind the redoubt towards the village of Hastenbeck	
Brunswick Leib-Regiment	2 Battalions
Brunswick Regiment Behr	2 Battalions

Reserve at Afferde which made sorties from behind Schekenberg	
Oberst von Dachenhausen, commander of the Hanoverian cavalry, east of Afferde.	
Regiment Schlütter	2 Squadrons
Regiment Dachenhausen	2 Squadrons

Oberst von Breidenbach, commander of a Hanoverian detachment north of Schekenberg between Afferde and Diedersen who made sorties into the Bisperod valley	
Breidenbach Dragoons	2 Squadrons
Regiment Sporcken	1 Battalion
Regiment Zandré de Caraffa	1 Battalion
Regiment Hardenberg	1 Battalion

Appendix VI

Formation of the Head of the Column which Attacked the Hastenbeck Woods

From the papers of the Marquis de Valfons

M. Éparvier (wounded), *lieutenant* of grenadiers of Picardie with 36 grenadiers made up of three from each company below, formed the small vanguard. 16 killed or wounded.

M. de Lauret (wounded), *capitaine* of Picardie grenadiers with his company * (3rd company of Picardie grenadiers). The *lieutenant* killed, the *sous-lieutenant* wounded, 20 grenadiers killed or wounded.

<u>M. de Sebourg, Marquis de Valfons, *major-général*; Comte du Chatelet (wounded), *colonel* of Navarre; M. Gascoing (killed), *lieutenant-colonel* of Picardie.</u>

Capitaine d'Urre (wounded), 1st company of Picardie grenadiers. 15 grenadiers, a *sergent* and the *lieutenant* killed.

Capitaine Dallenne (wounded), 2nd company of grenadiers of Picardie. 16 grenadiers killed and the lieutenant wounded.

Capitaine Caupenne (wounded), 1st company of grenadiers of Navarre. 19 grenadiers, 2 *sergents*, the *sous-lieutenant* and the *lieutenant* killed.

Capitaine d'Ablancourt (killed), 2nd company of grenadiers if Navarre. 8 grenadiers and the *lieutenant* killed.

Capitaine Lavie (killed), 3rd company of grenadiers of Navarre. 15 grenadiers, a *sergent* and the *lieutenant* killed.

Capitaine Darnans (wounded), 1st company of grenadiers of La Marine. 15 grenadiers and the *sous-lieutenant* killed.

Capitaine de Camps (killed), 2nd company of grenadiers of La Marine. 20 grenadiers, a *sergent* and the *lieutenant* killed.

Capitaine de Vignacourt (wounded), 3rd company of grenadiers of La Marine. 12 grenadiers, a *sergent* and the *lieutenant* killed.

Capitaine Grezian (wounded), 1st company of grenadiers of d'Eu. 14 grenadiers, a *sergent*, the *sous-lieutenant* and the *lieutenant* killed.

Capitaine d'Ortan (killed), 2nd company of grenadiers of d'Eu. 16 grenadiers, 2 *sergents* and the *lieutenant* killed.

Capitaine de Lammerville, 1st company of grenadiers of d'Enghien. 12 grenadiers, a *sergent* and the *lieutenant* killed.

* Each battalion had a company of grenadiers, i.e. four companies per brigade and a total of 16 companies for the entire column, 12 of which were in the vanguard. The grenadier compagnies of 4/Picardie, 4/Navarre, 4/La Marine and 2/Enghien remained with their battalion. The theoretical full strength of a company was 40 men, and it is reasonable to estimate their strength had reduced by 20 percent since leaving France, so roughly 32 men excluding officers.

Appendix VII

French Losses from the Battle of Hastenbeck

According to the report the King received on the loss of his troops at the Battle of Hastenbeck, there were seventeen officers killed & one hundred and eighteen wounded. The number of soldiers killed amounted to one thousand and thirty-eight, and the wounded to eleven hundred and fifty-nine.[1]

Staff

Killed: Comte de Montmorency-Laval, *colonel* of the Régiment de Guyenne serving as *aide-maréchal général des logis*.

Chevert's Column (Far Right)

Volontaires Royaux: 'commanded by M. de Bussy, killed by eight musket wounds, and 10 officers including 2 killed were wounded. 160 soldiers killed or wounded.'[2]

Volontaires de Flandre et de Hainaut: '6 officers killed or wounded; 120 soldiers killed or wounded.'[3]
Killed: M. de Beaussort, *lieutenant*.
Wounded: M. de Goussu, *capitaine,* shot through the ankle. M. de Boisgelin, *capitaine*, a finger shot away; M. de Schwartz, *lieutenant*, wounded in the arm; M. de Courtereille, *lieutenant*, wounded in the thigh.

Régiment de Picardie (4 Battalions): Around 300 killed or wounded.
Officers killed: M. de Gascoing, *lieutenant-colonel*.

---

1 *Gazette*, no.33 of 13 August 1757.
2 Valfons, *Souvenirs du marquis de Valfons*, annexe.
3 Valfons, *Souvenirs du marquis de Valfons*, annexe.

Officers wounded: Marquis de Bréhant, *colonel*, considerable contusion to one thigh; Chevalier d'Urre, *capitaine* of grenadiers, shot in the hand; M. Le Rique Dallenne, *capitaine* of grenadiers, shot in the shoulder; Chevalier de Saint-Mauris, *capitaine*, two bruises on his arm and foot; M. Durond, *capitaine*, two bruises on one leg; M. Panisson, *capitaine*, two shots in the head and in the arm; M. de Saint-Paul, *capitaine*, contusion on his foot; M. Dugravier, *capitaine*, shot in the leg; M. l'Eparvier, *lieutenant* of grenadiers, shot in the groin; M. Mondon, *lieutenant* of grenadiers, shot in the eye; M. du Molant, *lieutenant*, shot to the body; M. de Longchamp, *sous-lieutenant*, shot in the foot; M. de Vanteaux, *sous-lieutenant*, shot in the thigh.

Régiment de Navarre (4 Battalions):
Officers killed: M. d'Ablancourt, *capitaine* of grenadiers; M. de Lavie, grenadier *capitaine*, one leg shattered by a gunshot & M. de Fortenil, *lieutenant* of grenadiers, gunshot in the lower abdomen, dead from their wounds.
Officers wounded: Comte du Châtelet, *colonel*, gunshot in the lower abdomen; M. d'Orthez, assistant *capitaine*, shot in the arm; M. Le Frus, *capitaine aide-major*, shot in the foot; M. du Bortier, *capitaine*, bayonet stab to the leg; M. de Cassabé, *capitaine*, shot in the thigh; M. de Bonce, *capitaine*, shot in the chest; M. de Coquabanne, *capitaine*, shot in the foot; M. de Marqueta, *lieutenant*, shot to the shoulder; M. de Loisy, *lieutenant*, shot to the head; M. du Retard, *lieutenant*, shot in the arm; M. Petit, *sous-lieutenant*, shot in the leg; Chevalier de Saint-Segros, *volontaire*, hand pierced by a musket ball.

Régiment de La Marine (4 Battalions): Around 400 killed or wounded.
Officers killed: M. de Camps, *capitaine* of grenadiers; Chevalier des Augiers, *capitaine*; M. de la Plaine, *lieutenant* of grenadiers.
Officers Wounded: M. de Vignacourt, *capitaine* of grenadiers, shattered shoulder; Count de Darnans, *capitaine* of grenadiers, shot in the chest; M. de Ternol, *capitaine*, shot in the leg; MM. Broves and de la Cocherie, *capitaines*, shot in the arms; M. de Blaincourt, *capitaine*, contusion on his shoulder; M. de Gourdon, *capitaine aide-major*, shot in the foot; M. de Madaillant, *lieutenant*, bayonet stab in the leg.

Régiment d'Eu (2 Battalions): Around 400 killed or wounded from the two regiments of Eu and Enghien which formed a brigade.
Officers killed: Chevalier d'Ortan, *capitaine* of grenadiers; M. Darparens, *lieutenant* of grenadiers; M. Lenoble, *lieutenant*.
Officers wounded: M. de Grezian, *capitaine* of grenadiers, shot in the lower abdomen; M. du Chatelet, *capitaine*, shot in the leg; M. de l'Etang, *capitaine*, shot in the thigh; M. Pellagrue, *capitaine*, shot through the body; MM. Desmazis & de La Borie, *capitaines*, shot in the head; M. de Reynol, *capitaine*, shot in the shoulder; Chevalier de Singlande, *capitaine*, contusion to the thigh; Mr. Brosser, *capitaine*, knee contusion. M. Mousquerre, *capitaine*, wounded in the head; M. de Longpré,

lieutenant, shot through the body; M. de Barran, *lieutenant*, shot in the leg; M. de Saint-Quentin, *lieutenant*, shot to the head. MM. des Gatigny & d'Anfreville, *lieutenants*, shot in the legs; M. de Segla, *lieutenant*, flesh-wound; M. Jaoul, *lieutenant*, shot in the arm; M. Petitot, *lieutenant*, shot in the thigh.

Régiment de Enghien (2 Battalions): Around 400 killed or wounded from the two regiments of Eu and Enghien which formed a brigade.
Officer killed: MM. Rigolet de Saint-Pons & d'Orcin de Miraval, *capitaines* of grenadiers.
Officers wounded: M. de La More, *capitaine*, shot in the lower abdomen; M. de Bressay, *capitaine*, broken arm and gunshot to the back; M. de Grandvillars, *capitaine*, broken arm; M. De Mepieu, *capitaine*, kidney contusion; M. de Tournefort, *capitaine*, wounded in the head; M. de Beaumont, *capitaine*, two light blows to the head; M. Démont, *capitaine*, contusion in the thigh; Chevalier Rochon de La Pérouse, *major*, his horse overturned under him from a cannon shot; MM. de Vesigny & de Foucard, *capitaines aide-major*, the first with a shot in the thigh and his horse killed under him & the second wounded in the leg bone; MM. de Pracontal & de Grammont, *assistant majors*, the first to the thigh & the second with a gunshot to the ear; Chevalier de Grammont, *lieutenant*, wounded in the shoulder and head; M. Dassy, *lieutenant*, shot in the back; M. Bois de Bresy, *lieutenant*, shots to the head and lower abdomen; M. de Bec-de-Lièvre, *lieutenant*, shot through both shoulders; M. de Saint-Félix, *lieutenant*, contusion in the thigh; M. de Gouyon, *lieutenant*, shot in the shoulder; M. de Marchais, *lieutenant*, a broken thigh; MM. de Saint-Bry & de Boulot, *sous-lieutenants*, each wounded in the leg.

Marquis d'Armentières' Column (right)

Régiment de Belzunce (4 Battalions):
Officers killed: M. Regnaud, *capitaine*.
Officers wounded: Vicomte de Belzunce, *colonel*, shot in the arm; M. de Combas, *capitaine*, slightly injured; M. de Chapoton, *lieutenant* of grenadiers, contusion to the thigh; MM. D'Arbalestier and de Seimes, *lieutenants*, slightly injured.

Régiment de La Couronne (2 Battalions): 2 officers and 20 grenadiers killed.
Officers killed: M. de Miègeville *lieutenant* of grenadiers, M. de la Rocque, *volontaire*.

Régiment d'Alsace (3 Battalions):
Officers wounded: M. d'Atheim, *capitaine* of grenadiers, shot through the neck; Mr. Pigenot, *capitaine*, shot through the thigh; M. de Kellemback, *capitaine*, shot in the shoulder & cheek; Mr. Junck, *lieutenant* in grenadiers, shot to the shoulder; Mr. Koek, *lieutenant*, ditto.

APPENDIX VII

Marquis d'Anlézy's Column (Reserve)

Régiment de Champagne (4 Battalions): 3 officers and 63 non-commissioned officers and soldiers killed, around 80 wounded.
Officers killed: M. du Valon, *lieutenant*; MM. the *capitaines* de Francourt, his leg cut off, and Langle, shot through the body, died of their wounds.
Officers wounded: M. Domartin, *capitaine*, shot in the cheek; M. de Marsaing, *capitaine*, contusion on the arm from a bullet; M. Fauze, *capitaine*, contusion in the leg; M. de La Grange, *lieutenant*, contusion in the thigh.

Régiment de Reding (2 Battalions):
Officers wounded: M. Bilthener, *capitaine*, shot through the thigh; M. Voytel, *lieutenant*, contusion.

Régiment de Salis (2 Battalions):
Officers wounded: M. Salutz the elder, contusion.

Marquis de Contades' Column (Centre)

Régiment du Roy (4 Battalions):
Officers wounded: M. de Saintenac, *major*, contusion on his side; Chevalier de Raymond & M. de Sorbon, *capitaines*, similarly; M. Henu, *lieutenant*, one arm blown off.

Régiment de Mailly (4 Battalions):
Officers wounded: M. du Renaud, *capitaine*, in the arm by a cannon ball; M. de Montbel, *capitaine*, slightly injured in the knee; M. de Vendières, *capitaine*, in hand; M. de La Molère, *capitaine*, dangerously injured in the shoulder; M. du Bosse, *capitaine*, injured in the side; M. de Rochereul, *lieutenant*, dangerously injured in the armpit; MM. de Burthel and Buret, *lieutenants*, one on the leg, the other on the thigh.

Régiment de Vaubécourt (2 Battalions):
Officer killed: M. Mouroignon, *lieutenant*.
Officers wounded: M. de Baille, *capitaine*, cannon shot in the kidneys; M. de La Sablière, *capitaine*, one foot carried away; M. de La Menaye, *lieutenant*, cannon shot in the chest.

Comte de Guerchy (Centre)

Grenadiers Royaux de Solar (2 battalions):
Officers wounded: M. du Marché, *capitaine*, wounded in the chest; M. Richard, *capitaine*, knocked down by a ball but untouched; M. de Poncet, *aide-major*, wounded in the arm.

Duc de Broglie's Reserve (Left)

'In this reserve there were 38 men killed and 36 wounded'.[4]

Régiment de Provence (2 battalions):
Officer wounded: M. de Caupenne, *capitaine,* shot in the arm.

Régiment Royal-Suédois (2 battalions):
Officer killed: M. Dahestiern, *lieutenant.*
Officer wounded: M. de Dalhielm, *capitaine,* contusion on the head.

---

4 Duc de Broglie to the minister in Duteil, *Une famille militaire au XVIIIe siècle*, p.59.

Appendix VIII

Memoir of the Comte de Maillebois and Clarifications Presented to the King by *Maréchal* d'Estrées

On his return to France, the Comte de Maillebois tried to shake off the rumour that he had tried to disrupt the Battle of Hastenbeck. This was based on the official battle report which detailed misinformation from a 'trusted general officer' who delayed the final attack by half an hour. Maillebois drew up an anonymous supporting statement aimed at discrediting *Maréchal* d'Estrées. This attack was launched at an inopportune moment in 1758, when d'Estrées enjoyed the favour of the public and was once again in the good-graces of the King, and so this denunciation ended up working against him.

Maréchal d'Estrées had made his reconnaissance before crossing the Weser alone, leaving his *chef d'état-major* behind. The Comte de Maillebois had known the *Maréchal* was to be replaced from 7 July and had addressed his congratulations to the Duc de Richelieu who received them on the 14th.[1] It is therefore possible that the Comte wished to postpone any decisive action until the arrival of his favoured new commander-in-chief. If his conduct throughout the campaign was ambiguous, his behaviour during combat was more a loss of *sang-froid* than willingness to cause harm to the point of losing the battle.

The following is an extract from the memoirs of the Duc de Luynes which recounts the circumstances of the case between *Maréchal* Duc d'Estrées and the Comte de Maillebois:

> It was only a few days ago that M. le *Maréchal* de Maillebois sent to the King a memoire from his son, and M. de Maillebois junior delivered it to M. de Puisieux

---

[1] 'I received a letter from the Minister, who confided to me on behalf of the King, and to me alone, the new assignment of M. le Maréchal de Richelieu, & the reunion of the army intended for him with that of M. le Maréchal d'Estrées. This letter is dated 2 July ... I received it on the 7th.' *Memoire de Maillebois*, p.8.

personally. This last step was unbelievable; for, although M. de Maillebois assured M. de Puisieux that he had written nothing against the honour of M. le *Maréchal* d'Estrées, his [Pusieux's] son-in-law, one only needs to read the memorandum to be fully convinced to the contrary. The main object of this memoir concerned a notice given to *Maréchal* d'Estrées at the end of the battle of Hastenbeck which was thought to persuade him to retire in the midst of his victory. It was to warn him that he would be cut down by enemy troops sent through the woods. This news was found to be entirely false, and it was judged that whoever it came from would have been very wicked to imagine it or would seem to be totally wrong if they had been persuaded of it. It has been claimed that it was M. de Maillebois that sent this message, though he maintains in his memoir that he never said or thought it; he even claimed he was not on the flank from which the advice is claimed to have come; finally, to prove that far from wanting to diminish the glory of *Maréchal* d'Estrées, he took on a large number of operations of this campaign before the battle, and gave judgment, by the details he wrote, that the passage from the Weser, which was followed until the moment of the battle, and the very arrangement made for this battle, were the continuation of advice he himself had given to *Maréchal* d'Estrées and arrangements he had made. One cannot undertake such a project without generally assuming irresolution and lack of knowledge; and these two articles are explained quite clearly by the terms of the said memorandum. M. de Maillebois wanted M. de Puisieux to keep the memorandum for examination, but M. de Puisieux, after having read it, assured him that he would not wish to touch such a paper, and that the only prudent and wise thing to do would be not to tell his son-in-law about it. In fact, he ignored this memoir that had been communicated to him. However, M. le *Maréchal* de Maillebois handed it over to his nephew, M. de Bercy, who reported the affair in its entirety to the *tribunal de maréchaux de France*. M. de Bercy read to this court in the presence of M. le Maréchal d'Estrées. The matter appeared to deserve the greatest attention, in relation to the maintenance of subordination and discipline. It seems that we must consider it essential not to allow an inferior officer the freedom to decry the conduct of his general, a *Maréchal de France* in public. We still do not know which side we will take; the memoir is in the hands of Maréchal de Belle-Isle, who will report on it to His Majesty … *Maréchal* d'Estrées thought it his duty to respond to M. de Maillebois's brief, but he behaved in a very different manner; he wrote a memoir in which he explained the facts with truth and simplicity, and had it delivered to the King. This memoir was read to the *tribunal de maréchaux de France* by order of the King, and H.M. was so pleased with it that not only did he allow, but even ordered *Maréchal* d'Estrées to have it printed. This memoir has not yet been seen by the public, it has only been published today after printing.[2]

---

2   Duc de Luynes, *Memoires du duc de Luynes*, Vol.XVI, pp.441-442.

Select Bibliography

Published Sources

Albert, *Capitaine* Augustin François Marie, *Recueil de faits pour servir à l'histoire militaire du corps des Carabiniers* (Paris: Guibal, 1814).

Aunillon, Pierre, *Gazette*. Paris, n°14 and n°33, from 2 avril to 13 août 1757.

Besenval, Pierre Victor baron de, *Mémoires du baron de Bésenval* (Paris: Baudouin, 1821).

Bonal, *Colonel* François, *Les régiments de Champagne sous l'Ancien Régime* (Langres: Guéniot, 1999).

Buvignier-Cloüet, Madeleine, *Chevert lieutenant-général des armées du roi 1695-1769* (Paris: Renvé-Lallemant, 1888).

Chevrier, François Antoine, *Histoire de la campagne de mil sept cent cinquante-sept sur le Bas-Rhin dans l'Électorat d'Hanovre et autres pays conquis* (Francfort: Unknown Publisher, 1757).

Du Bois, *Camps topographiques de la campagne de 1757 en Westphalie* (Paris: Veuve Van Duren, 1760). Du Bois was the geographical engineer of the Comte de Maillebois.

Dziembowski, Edmond, *La guerre de Sept ans* (Paris: Perrin, 2015).

Desbrière, *Commandant* Édouard & Sautai, *Capitaine* Maurice, *La cavalerie de 1740 à 1789* (Paris: Berger-Levrault, 1906).

Duteil, Joseph Baron, *Une famille militaire au XVIIIe siècle* (Paris: Picard, 1896).

Estrées, Louis Charles César Le Tellier, *Maréchal d'*, *Éclaircissements présentés au roi* (Paris: Simon, 1758).

Hardy de Périni, *Colonel* Édouard, *Batailles françaises, VI – les armées sous l'Ancien Régime* (Paris: Flammarion, 1906).

Hubner, Jean, *La géographie universelle* (Paris: Jean Rodolphe, 1757).

Jomini, *Chef de Bataillon* Antoine Henri, *Traité de grande tactique* (Paris: Magimel, 1805).

Jomini, Antoine Henri Baron de, *Histoire critique et militaire des guerres de Frédéric II* (Brussels: Petit, 1842).

Koch, Christophe Guillaume, *Histoire abrégée des traités de paix entre les puissances de l'Europe depuis la paix de Westphalie* (Paris: Gide fils, 1817).

Lainé, P. Louis, *Archives généalogiques et historiques de la noblesse de France* (Paris: Lainé, 1828-1850).

Luynes, Charles-Philippe d'Albert Duc de, *Mémoires du duc de Luynes sur la Cour de Louis XV* (Paris: Firmin-Didot, 1864).

Maillebois, Yves Marie Desmarets, Comte de, *Mémoire du comte de Maillebois* (Amsterdam: Unknown Publisher, 1758).

Montandre, Chevalier de, *État militaire de France pour l'année 1759.* (Paris: Guillyn, 1759).

Mopinot de la Chapotte, Antoine Rigobert, *Sous Louis le Bien-Aimé. — correspondance amoureuse et militaire d'un officier pendant la guerre de Sept-ans (1757-1765)* (Paris: Calmann-Lévy, 1905).

Napoléon 1er, *Précis des guerres de Frédéric II, commentaires sur la guerre de Sept ans* (Réédition: Amazon, 2018).

Pajol, Charles Pierre Victor Comte, *Les guerres sous Louis XV* (Paris: Firmin-Didot, 1885).

Poli, Vicomte Oscar de, *Le régiment de la Couronne (1643- 1791)* (Paris: Conseil héraldique de France, 1891).

Retzow, F.A. von, *Nouveaux mémoires historiques sur la guerre de Sept ans Traduits de l'Allemand* (Paris: Treuttel et Würtz, 1803).

Pinard, François-Joseph-Guillaume, *Chronologie historique militaire* (Paris: Onfroy, 1778).

Rocquancourt, *Chef d'escadron, Cours complet d'art et d'histoire militaires à l'usage des élèves de l'École royale spéciale militaire* (Paris: Anselin, 1841).

Roussel, M. de, *Essais historiques sur les régiments d'infanterie, cavalerie et dragons* (Paris: Guillyn, 1765-1767).

Roussel, M. de. *Table historique de l'état militaire de France depuis 1758 jusqu'à présent* (Paris: Guillyn, 1766).

Rousset, Camille, *Le comte de Gisors (1732-1758), étude historique* (Paris: Didier, 1868)

Valfons, Charles de Mathei Marquis de, *Souvenirs du marquis de Valfons, vicomte de Sebourg, lieutenant-général des armées du Roi (1710-1786)* (Émile Paul, 1907).

Vogüé, Marquis de & Le Sourd, Auguste, *Campagnes de Jacques de Mercoyrol de Beaulieu, capitaine au régiment de Picardie* (Renouard: Société de l'histoire de France, 1915).

Waddington, Richard, *La guerre de Sept ans, histoire diplomatique et militaire. — Les débuts* (Firmin-Didot, 1899).

Manuscripts

Service historique de la défense (SHD). *Journal de la campagne de 1757*. Archives du génie. Série 1 V, article 15, section 1, dossier 5, pièce 23. Vincennes.

Service historique de la défense (SHD). *Correspondance, année 1757*. Série A1, Ancien Régime, registre 3436, pièces 113 à 124. Vincennes.